Dreamers
Never Sleep

Pat Mesiti

Dreamers Never Sleep
Copyright © 1996 Pat Mesiti
Educational, Motivational

ISBN 0 64626624 1

Typeset by Your Image
17 Ancilia Close
Quakers Hill NSW 2763

Cover design by CPGD
4 Marguerite Crescent
West Pennant Hills NSW 2125

Printed in Australia by
Pirie Printers Pty Limited
140 Gladstone Street
(PO Box 438) Fyshwick ACT 2609

Printed in United States of America by
KNI , Incorporated
1261 S. State College Parkway
Anaheim, Ca 92806

ACKNOWLEDGEMENTS

First of all I would like to thank my wife, Liz, and my two daughters, Rebecca and Chantelle, for the constant joy and love that they give me. Their encouragement is immeasurable and their dedication to the dream is a continual source of motivation.

Super huge thanks to Craig Hingston, the only person I know who can interpret Italian shorthand and turn my thoughts and notes into words that work. Thanks for your literary assistance. You've done it again!

To my best friends, Brian and Bobbie Houston, thank you for always being there and for your friendship that has often gone beyond the call of duty.

To Graeme Kirkwood: you are a faithful man and that is the most worthy of all character traits.

To Kylie Taylor: thank you for a faithful five years; to Lyn Ollis and Tania Campbell: thanks for all the extra hours and hard work. Keep the fire going; to Mike Cowdroy: keep chasing your dreams; to the board at Youth Alive and the team at Hills Christian Life Centre: a special thanks to you all. Also to Joy McCarthy and Owen Salter.

Lastly, and most importantly, thank you to you for reading this book. Readers are a writer's dream.

18 Principles To Help You Discover Your Purpose In Life

PART THREE
*THE OBSTACLES, CHALLENGES
AND HINDRANCES*

PART FOUR
BECOMING THE BETTER YOU

INTRODUCTION

"That's it! I give up! I'm doing the best I can and if my best isn't good enough that's too bad."

How often have you heard those words - possibly out of your own mouth? They mostly come from people attempting to achieve a certain goal or task who haven't succeeded yet. Perhaps you're making progress, getting closer and closer to the mark, but as far as you're concerned you've reached the limit of your potential. You can't go another step.

Is it really your very best? Or simply your best for today? There's more potential within than you give yourself credit for.

The object of this book is to show you that what you consider to be your best is simply the latest level you've reached in your journey through life. You can become better. How well you perform today has no bearing on how you can be in a year's time. Or two years.

Life is an endless progression, and so is success. It involves going from one stage to the next. I want to take you on a journey of the bigger and better You. I want you to drop your guard and put aside any preconceived ideas you might have that will hinder this self-discovery or stop the release of your dormant potential.

I'm going to lay some ideas out for you and challenge you. The biggest favour you can do for yourself is to take hold of the spirit of this book: *you are created for far greater things*. What I've written is not intended to make you relax and accept mediocrity. It's meant to get you up on your feet, out of "Cruise Control" and into the starting blocks, then to propel you like an arrow towards your destiny. To go out there and change your world - and the worlds of others.

I want you to find me after one of our Youth Alive rallies or business functions, write to me, call me, fax me or send a carrier pigeon and tell me that you have started out as a pioneer. I want you to tell me that you're trailblazing along the most exciting adventure of all: your life.

In my last book, *Wake Up And Dream*, I encouraged you to believe in your dream. This book takes you to the next step, the substance it takes to fulfil your dream.

Will your betterment be a smooth highway? I doubt it. More like a bumpy off-road car rally through the bush! Let's be honest: you're going to have challenges and struggles. They're a part of learning and moving on.

But I hope that this book will inspire you to make the decision to wake up and win. Go the extra mile. Dare to excel. Become the best You that you can be.

LET'S GO!

PAT MESITI

PART ONE
THE FIRST STEPS
TOWARDS BETTERMENT

1. Replacing Wrong Perceptions With Winning Attitudes
2. Making Friends With Change
3. Bend And S-T-R-E-T-C-H-H-H
4. A Dreamer Looks Like You
5. Success...It's Your Choice
6. Always Let Your Conscience Be Your Guide

"If I lost my talent tomorrow I'd say I had a great time and move on. I live for today but plan for the future."
Michael Jordan

1.
REPLACING WRONG PERCEPTIONS WITH WINNING ATTITUDES

"You and I do not see things as they are, we see things as we are."
Herb Cohen

Before you start anything in life you are going to have to confront a very powerful influence: your preconceived ideas. How you think about life, yourself, your abilities, your family and friends is moulding you.

Famous motivational speaker Zig Ziglar put it this way: "You can't consistently perform in a manner that is inconsistent with the way you see yourself." James Allen took this a step further: "You are today where your thoughts have brought you, you will be tomorrow where your thoughts take you." And I recall reading a personal development book once which stated:

If you THINK you are beaten you are,
If you THINK you dare not you don't,
If you'd like to win but THINK you can't, it's almost certain you won't.

"Our attitude toward things is likely to be more important than the things themselves."
A. W. Tozer

Think about it. What is your perception of yourself? Do you consider yourself to be good looking? Well groomed? Talented? Positive? Worthy of success? What are your thoughts towards others - your family and relatives, peers, workmates, neighbours or employer? What do you think of people who are more successful than you? Do you believe that you have a special one-off destiny awaiting you which only you can fulfil? The thoughts you have about these things are controlling you. How you view the world controls your progress. It's a daunting thought.

Your perceptions are so powerful that they will limit the level of progress and success that you feel worthy of achieving. Regardless of previous experience, skills, product quality, advertising or hard work, self-esteem is the limiter.

If you are willing to focus on changing your preconceptions, the success principles throughout the rest of this book will be so much easier to adopt and develop.

"We can do things we don't even dream we can do." Dale Carnegie

The Day I Met The Wall With Hair
I recall one time when I fell victim to prejudging people. It was the day I met the Wall With Hair.

The scene was in New Zealand. I was speaking in high schools and some Maori elders asked me to talk to a group of their people at their *marae* (their sacred ground).

Let me tell you something about these beautiful Maori people. When they sing it seems like heaven has turned up on earth. What voices! What harmonies! And they are so giving and loving, nothing is ever too hard for them. However, I didn't know this as I walked into the main building and immediately noticed half a dozen guys sitting in the back row. Actually, they weren't human. They were walls. They made Arnold Schwarzenneger look average. Not only were they huge, they were ugly. Each one had tattoos across his face like Spiderman, a nose wider than the Grand Canyon and lips that would make Mick Jagger jealous.

They sat with their arms folded and glared at me as I started to speak. Something inside told me they were not Sunday School teachers. I later found out they were members of the fearsome Black Power motorbike gang.

As I talked I developed a mindset about these guys. They didn't like me, I decided. Their body language said aggressive, intolerant. And I wasn't sure that the topic for my presentation - Purpose - was all that relevant to them either.

The more I spoke the more annoyed I became because of my preconceptions.

I reached the end of my message — *phew!* — bowed my head and prayed. I prayed one prayer for them and another silent one for myself, something about surviving the meeting and making it home to my wife and daughters in one piece. Then I challenged the people who wanted a fresh start in life to come up to the front so that I could talk to them.

That was when I felt the earth move. I know New Zealand is right in an earthquake zone but this was a different tremor. This one had legs. I felt like I was in a scene from *Jurassic Park*. I noticed the glass of water on the podium moving with each rumble.

I looked up and there was the biggest and meanest part of the Wall With Hair bearing down on me. I had a sudden urge to hide under the furniture or run for the bathroom. He stopped and suddenly I was staring at his belly button. "It's been nice knowing me," I thought.

Then a funny thing happened. The belly button started quivering as the surrounding stomach started heaving up and down. He was sobbing. Then that big, tough bikie bowed his head and mumbled, "Sir, I want some o' dat."

"Some of what?" I asked, stunned.

"Some o' dat what you talked about. Por-poise."

"What?"

"Por-poise."

Purpose, por-poise, I wasn't about to argue. When you're confronted by a seven-foot, 400-pound Maori, spelling isn't an issue. Life is - your own.

"I need help," he continued as sobs melted into tears.

My heart turned to marshmallow and I tried to hug him but my little arms only went halfway around his big waist. He wrapped his long tentacles around me and squeezed my face into his tummy. He cried, I cried, everybody cried. It was a special, tender moment as this person discovered he had something to live for and decided to pursue it.

We went back to his house and had fried bread and pork bones - a Maori delicacy - and he opened up and shared his life with me. He was the leader of a gang. They had committed some hideous crimes and most of his mates were in jail. Yet that night his life was changed. He found his "por-poise".

A while later I was back in a local school speaking to young people when, all of a sudden, the Wall With Hair showed up. Had the gang leader changed his mind? Had he decided to do me in for embarrassing him in front of his mates? No. He asked me to go to the maximum security prison where his friends were and speak to them. Fortunately he was able to break through their preconceptions about this short funny Italian from Australia and they also opened up to me. The guys are still there, but I can tell you that on the inside they have become free.

The point I want to make is that at first I allowed tattoos, scars, broken teeth, unwashed hair, black leather jackets and body language to control my thoughts. When I put them aside, destiny was able to take over.

Wrong Perceptions Deny Destiny
The same principle applies to every area of life. Whether it is a business proposal or getting someone involved with your social club, people do not always have the negative attitudes you think. Change your perceptions.

Why go out, for example, and show business plans to people when you're already convinced they won't become a part of it? You've conditioned your mindset before you've tried. At worst a person will say no, at best they'll join up and do well.

The Bible has an interesting story about wrong perceptions denying people their true destiny. After the people of Israel were rescued from slavery in Egypt, they began crossing the dry, hot Sinai Desert. They were going back to the land which had been promised to their forefathers long before.

Moses sent twelve spies to check out the "Promised Land" before they marched in and took it. It's amazing what happened. Ten spies returned in absolute fear saying it was impossible to possess the land. The inhabitants were tall, muscular people with fortified cities and sophisticated weaponry.

"We were like grasshoppers in our own eyes and in theirs," they whined.

While panic set in across the encampment, spies eleven and twelve, Joshua and Caleb, returned with big smiles across their faces. They talked of huge crops and an abundance of livestock — a land of milk and honey. Sure, the locals were tough guys, but the Israelites could beat them. After all, they had just been miraculously delivered from the most powerful nation on earth. This was going to be easy!

Sadly, gross exaggeration and pessimism won the day, and most of the Israelites never saw their destiny. Instead, they wasted four decades wandering aimlessly around and around that dust bowl. Only two men lived to see Israel conquer their Promised Land. You guessed it: Joshua and Caleb.

The Power Of One
Attitudes and mindsets control life. For example, one reason why our world is in such turmoil and grief is because people have the mindset that they don't want to step out and help others. They don't want to go the extra mile or make the needy a priority in life. A great many people are self-centred: take care of Number One and forget the rest.

Another wrong mindset is that people believe their life has no significance. "What can I do, I'm only one person?"

Do you realise that the dream of an individual can make life better for multitudes? One is a big number when you have a destiny and are determined to reach it.

Winston Churchill was one man and he brought courage and steadfastness to a battered country during the Second World War. I've been told that when Adolf Hitler listened to Churchill's

When wrong perceptions are replaced by winning attitudes, anything can happen.

speech saying the British would fight in the streets and on the beaches to save their homeland, he had second thoughts about invading Britain. The attitude of one man passed on to an entire nation and helped create history.

Nelson Mandela is one person and he changed the mindset of an entire nation. I visited South Africa not long ago, and while I was at a restaurant with friends, a beautiful black waitress with the biggest smile came and served us. We watched how she worked with evident joy and dignity. Her attitude was more than that of a "humble waitress". It had gone from oppression to opportunity.

As we left I asked if they accepted tips. She beamed, "Yes, sir, this is the new South Africa."

I responded accordingly.

Being armed with a list of dreams and step-by-step goals is not enough. All the best intentions in the world will not amount to anything unless you allow yourself to be "reprogrammed" for victory. Replace your wrong perceptions with winning attitudes.

Bull In A Steakhouse
A few years ago I was asked to speak to students at a high school. They all had preconceived ideas of what I looked like and what I was going to say. They were expecting a holier-than-thou tongue lashing from someone totally out of touch with young people.

I knew that the school was filled with racism, divided by religious beliefs, had an enormously high pregnancy rate and was in one of the worst economic areas in our city. On top of that, the senior class I was about to address was the most violent, crime-infested year in the school's history.

I stood at the back of the auditorium and watched the boys strut in like roosters in a hen house. Dark sunglasses, baseball caps on backwards, shirts hanging out. They transformed the previously tidy hall into a cross between a nuclear holocaust and their bedrooms. The girls had skirts so short a blind man could have seen them at midnight!

It did not start well. The first teacher got up on stage and said, "Good morning, you bunch of unteachables. Shut up and listen to what this man wants to teach you." I was sure he had been a sergeant-major before being a teacher.

The second teacher was a cross between Mother Goose and Alice in Wonderland. Her opening line was "Good morning, children". Let me tell you, streetwise and very cool teenagers do not like being referred to as children. I looked for the exit. She continued, "Mr Mesiti has come to share some precious thoughts with you this day. Give him a warm welcome, school."

The silence was deafening.

To say my reception was icy was an understatement. I felt as uncomfortable as a bull in a steakhouse and a termite in a yo-yo. They were ready to eat me alive.

I knew these young people had preconceived ideas about me and I was about to blow them sky high. The first thing I did was make them laugh. The second thing I did was make them laugh. The third thing I did... As a matter of fact, I think that's all I did.

Then halfway through my talk I changed direction and the raucous laughter turned to silence. I started challenging them about values, morals, character and thinking about their future. "Young men, being a man is more than being born male. Young women, life is more than being used and abused."

The silence grew even louder.

As I covered such issues as hurt, loneliness and seeking identity, the steely faces softened, tears started to flow, then came loud sobs. I felt a lump in my throat the size of a golf ball.

When I finished my talk the senior year rose to their feet and gave me a standing ovation. I'd broken through. I felt like a champion being awarded his trophy. These wonderful young Australians had suddenly discovered what it means to live. They had put aside perceptions and found purpose.

The principal came running over and asked me if I wanted a job. I replied, "No thanks, I have a life!"

Who needs a job when you've got a mission!

How Well Do You Know Yourself?
What preconceived ideas do you have about yourself? In many cases, preconceptions aren't based on truth but on your *understanding* of the truth. For example, you might think you don't have any friends when in fact a lot of people around you enjoy your company but haven't come out and said so.

You may have dealt with a lot of challenges or heartaches in life. Those experiences can either make you or break you. Your mindset decides.

Perhaps you don't have the latest car or the nicest house in the street. You haven't bought clothes for years and your furniture is getting worn out. But the fact is that you can better yourself and improve your lifestyle—if you believe you can. Or perhaps you set up your own business and it failed, or married your sweetheart and it ended in divorce.

> *"My ability was twenty percent physical, eighty percent mental."*
> *Australian athlete*

Preconceptions might tell you it's useless to try again. But the fact is that the next enterprise or relationship you begin could be the breakthrough - if you believe it.

But you won't try unless your mindset is programmed to allow you. As one popular song says: Change your mind and the rest will follow.

Reprogramming Your Mind

I remember seeing an interview on television with a member of the Australian Commonwealth Games team just after he'd won gold. The question was how much of his ability was physical and how much mental. The response astounded me: "Twenty per cent physical, eighty per cent mental."

Over the years we've all built refuges in our minds and we retreat back into them when faced with a challenge. If we failed at something once before, our "computer" says, "You're no good at that" and we avoid it.

But like a computer, our minds can be reprogrammed. A good way to do this is with daily affirmations. I've spoken to a number of successful businessmen, some of whom are worth millions, who carry around small cards in their pockets with positive statements on them like "I can do..." and "I am a good..." and "I have..."

At present none of these people have fully achieved these things; but they are telling themselves that they have, and in time their minds believe it. It might sound crazy to you, but if by reading these affirmations each day they can reach their destinies, then I'm willing to do it too.

Is "reprogramming" simple? Can a victory mentality be achieved overnight? No! To some achievers this becomes a crisis. The only solution is: DON'T STOP! Have patience. Keep working at it. And remember, even the snail by perseverance reached Noah's Ark!

Don't fall asleep. Don't stop dreaming. Dreamers never sleep!

TAKE ACTION

1. Make a list of the preconceptions you have because of past experiences

...about yourself

...about your family and friends

...about your skills, talents, ability to learn and develop further

...about your worthiness to have an abundant and successful future

...about your ability to be loved and to make new relationships

2. Make a list of how you would ideally like to be in all of these areas.

3. What can you learn from comparing your preconceptions about yourself with your dreams?

A QUICK LOOK AT PRECONCEPTIONS

1. How you view yourself and the world controls your life and your progress.

2. You can change your preconceptions.

3. Don't judge others.

4. One person with a dream is very powerful.

5. Use daily self-talk to "reprogram" your mind:

"I am good at..."

"I do have..."

"I can do..."

2.
MAKING FRIENDS
WITH CHANGE

*"When you can't change
the direction of the wind,
change your sails."*
Max Depree

Dreamers change things, things don't change them. In other words, dreamers are catalysts of change for the better. They're not crippled by negative circumstances; they're launched by them.

I often ask people, "Are you a catalyst or a sponge?" There are big differences between the two.

SPONGE
• absorbs
• takes on the colour, odour and flavour of its environment
• gives in or succumbs to moods and fears, imagined or real
• does not bounce back
• outside forces dictate its reaction
• rehearses past hurts and failures, holds onto them

CATALYST
• emits
• changes its environment, is not poisoned or infiltrated by it
• mentally gains inner strength
• implements change
• acts on life
• goes anywhere, anytime
• does what has to be done to reach the goal

- sees life as a downward spiral

- is not crippled by criticism
- uses personal attacks and difficulties as building materials for building dreams

The message is: if you want to see change in your life, you're going to have to change something in your life.

I congratulate you on having the courage and determination to put past perceptions away and start afresh.

You might not understand everything about this new stage of progress. Don't worry. Have faith that you're on the right track.

"Unless we change our direction we are likely to end up where we are headed."
Chinese proverb

One Hundred Per Cent Predictable
Change and crisis aren't necessarily the same thing, but both are 100 per cent predictable. They will both occur in your lifetime, more than once. They are as predictable as gravity.

Nature is constantly changing. For example, cells in the human body are growing non-stop. Every minute of the day you are producing new skin cells, blood cells, hair and so on (although I think my hair regrowth has stopped!).

Our world is constantly changing. The ugly regime of apartheid has been dismantled, the walls of Euro-Communism have come tumbling down, economic power seems to be shifting to Asia. Or think about communications. At the beginning of this century, Marconi first used the wireless to transmit the spoken word around the world. What a breakthrough! Yet today we have an exploding information superhighway, from CD ROMs to the Internet. A person in the computer industry told me that knowledge is doubling every few years! Today's remote control, high speed, triple layer, hi-res, microchip product is obsolete as soon as it has been made.

Regardless of which endeavours you're involved in, all of them undergo change, development or refinement - sometimes on a day-to-day basis. When I'm talking to people in high schools, rallies, concerts or business seminars, I often say that life is a series of changes. That's why it's important to understand change.

Changes can be crises or springboards. Our attitudes determine which they are for us. First we must accept them, then we must use them.

Refusing Change
One of our generation's pop idols, Tori Amos, stated

in *Rolling Stone* magazine that our generation loves to complain, but it doesn't want to change anything, because if it changes things it will have nothing to complain about.

> *"The individuals who will succeed and flourish will also be the masters of change."*
> **R. Kanter**

Nothing changes until something changes. That may not seem profound, but think about it. I remember the first time I heard these words it suddenly hit me how true they were. When change is necessary and we refuse to allow it to take place or struggle against it, our stubbornness can be highly destructive. It can cause change to work against us and push us further behind in our walk through life.

Some time ago a colleague asked me to call a business associate of his. That person wanted me to speak to his employees on the subject of guilt. I phoned to make contact with this manager and get some background information which would help me prepare my talk.

I was curious why he had chosen the topic of guilt and I asked if he had problems with staff taking money from the cash register. No, came the reply. Were they falsifying time sheets? No. Fiddling the books? No. Taking unofficial sick leave or stealing from the warehouse? He answered no to everything. The obvious question was, "Is there any specific area related to guilt?"

It's a personal thing, answered the businessman, but he wanted it dealt with in a group environment, not one-to-one. Then he opened up and I learnt the real reason for the request. He said his work required a lot of travel and while he was away he was getting involved with other women.

I could sense he was after some kind of approval for his adultery but I hit him straight. "Rather than come out I'll save you a speaking fee and give you some free advice on how to handle it. Have you got pen and paper?"

"Yes."

"Good. Now write this down: I must stop doing what is causing the guilt."

There was a long pause. I knew he hadn't wanted this sort of advice, but his destructive behaviour was going to ruin him if he didn't stop.

Generally speaking, the majority of people are resistant to change. They prefer the status quo. It's comfortable. There isn't any unknown.

Yet our lives are in a constant process of change. In his book *Empires of the Mind*, Denis Waitley says,

"You must welcome change as the rule, but not as your ruler." Change is inevitable. It should serve you. It shouldn't crush, stifle or kill you; rather, it should launch you.

"One change makes way for the next giving us the opportunity to grow."
Vivien Buchen

Benefit From Change
As you analyse your life and where you want to go, consider the following points:

1. Is change necessary?

If things aren't going according to your plans it generally means something needs to change. As motivator and author Zig Ziglar says in *Over The Top*, "One definition of insanity is to believe that you can keep on doing what you've been doing and get different results."

2. How should things change?

Does your situation require dramatic, drastic change, or gradual, calculated change?

3. What needs to change first?

We need to prioritise change.

4. Realise that all change involves some kind of discipline and makes you a little uncomfortable.

For example, if you take sugar in your coffee and try going without it, at first it tastes awful. But keep drinking it and after a while you will get used to it.

Most change has a level of discomfort or pain, but it is only temporary. Athletes exercise, their bodies change, they develop more strength, more muscle. They go through dietary changes, mental changes, more exercise, more training. More change happens.

I believe we are like athletes. Change can be painful, it needs to be repetitive, and it produces growth and strength.

The only thing we need to fear from change, is not changing.

The right thing to do with change is to benefit from it. Move with the times. Don't be threatened by it; instead, see unlimited possibilities available to you through it.

(Of course, not all change is good. For example, some people today want to re-define the family and the roles and responsibilities of its members. If you want to destroy the power of something like the family unit, change its value and try to re-define it. Break apart the family and you break apart society. Change is very powerful - for good and bad.)

It's All In The Timing

The reason why change is a threat or crisis to some people is that it often requires more effort and work. There's a new learning curve as we re-educate ourselves. It can mean new responsibilities, new job profiles, a change as to how we treat people, customers, parishioners or team members.

Change means welcoming the new. Being open to the unseen, untried and untested.

That's why, as a rule, I prefer to make changes a step at a time. Like exercise, drastic movement can cause injury, yet calculated and gradual movement builds strength. Take each change of direction on its own merits. Some must be instantaneous while others can be phased in over an extended period of time.

> *"Most bold change is the result of 100,000 tiny changes."*
> *Thomas Peters*

In the workplace rapid change can unsettle employees, affecting productivity and morale. One positive alteration which has been filtering through the international business world is the philosophy of interdependence over independence. People are relying on each other, building on their strengths and operating more as a team.

Positives Of Change

People complain about all kinds of things. They

complain that the world is in a mess yet are unwilling to take the steps to change the factors in their life that contribute to making the world a miserable place. They complain about racism, the economy, injustice and the environment but are reluctant to change their own behaviour.

Don't consider change as negative or destabilising. Over the years I've seen many changes in my life lead to positives, usually in the following areas:

Change has got nothing to do with your age, and everything to do with your desired success.

1. Propelling into the future.

We are often able to use change to shoot us towards our destiny a lot faster than if the change had not occurred.

2. Preparing for the future.

Change can help us to assess things before they happen, as well as to consider possible rewards, opportunities and problems in the future and anticipate their arrival.

3. Providing for the future.

Change keeps us in business, on the Cutting Edge. Without it we would be condemned to relying on archaic systems and outdated communication. Change can force us to move with the times, keeping us efficient and profitable.

4. Producing a leaner and more efficient person.

Change often teaches us new skills and better ways of achieving our goals, thereby making us more efficient. Change educates, making us more informed, and rekindles the pioneering spirit that might have been lost in the busyness of life.

Change releases fresh leadership, concepts and ideas. At Youth Alive we pride ourselves on staging contemporary, hi-tech events, yet after one such concert I came to the shocking conclusion that the things we were doing weren't relating to young people of the '90s. We were still using late '80s-early '90s methods of music and dance. To remain relevant required change. Instead of repeating the stereotyped format at our next rally, we introduced new methods and styles. They were subtle, but the audience noticed.

"Change is the law of life."
John F. Kennedy

One of the dumbest mistakes we can make in life is to think we've made it. There is no need to make any more adjustments or changes, we'll just refine what we already know.

Change is positive in the business or sports environments because it doesn't look at who is to blame. It stimulates new ideas, seeks smarter ways of working and ultimately achieves better results.

Over the decades, Olympians have set times that people expected to remain unbroken for a long time. They were performing at then-known peaks of achievement. But coaching methods changed, exercise methods changed, the understanding of how the body works increased. Now blistering times are set and reset every four years. Similarly, with dramatic advances in technology, communication and business-building techniques, companies are making more money in the '90s than ever before, while the ones clinging to antiquated methods are being left behind.

Many people have made the choice to move ahead, written down their goals, then allowed excuses to overpower their dreams. Today they are full of regret, miles and miles from their destiny. If you have stayed in the starting blocks after the gun has gone off I have a word of encouragement for you. You might have missed the first heat, but the athletes are lining up for the second heat and you've still got an opportunity to put your excuses aside and GO FOR IT!

Don't be a "should have, could have, would have" person. Get ready for change. Welcome it. Because when things change it can be change for the better.

TAKE ACTION

1. What are the positives of change?

2. What positive results could change produce for your life?

3. Write down things you feel need to change in your life. They might include:

• Attitude (is your attitude what it should be? Remember, you choose your moods and outlook)
• Mindset (are you positive or negative? What things do you need to do to change the way you think?)
• Family (are you spending enough time with your partner, children and relatives? Do you show enough affection? If not, what small thing could you do to bring about an improvement?)
• Physical (are you where you should be with your weight? Cholesterol level? Shape? If not, why not? What would need to change? Your diet? Exercise?)

4. Set out an agenda of small steps you will need to take so that you can improve.

A QUICK LOOK AT ACCEPTING CHANGE

1. The only way to allow change in life is to change.

2. Dreamers effect change, change doesn't affect them.

3. Change is uncomfortable (but the effects of no change are far worse).

4. Change is totally natural.

5. Change releases fresh creativity and leadership.

6. To resist change can be destructive.

3.
BEND AND
S-T-R-E-T-C-H-H-H

*Those who don't take
chances don't make advances.
To progress, even the turtle
has to stick his neck out.*

The majority of people in the world today prefer to fall into "quit" mode. Take the easy way. Don't exert themselves. They curl up in the corner for a short nap which turns into a long rest then a deep sleep. But remember: Dreamers never sleep!

If you're really serious about becoming the best possible You, you're going to have to s-t-r-e-t-c-h-h. If you want to change something in your life, you have to change something in your life!

Stretching is a natural process; all of nature stretches and grows. But we humans have adopted a negative attitude to it. Rather than accept the challenges and pain of extending ourselves, most prefer to stop.

I can't explain it any simpler than this: If you refuse to stretch then get used to where you are at now, because that's where you're going to stay. While dreamers go racing down the swift currents of life, you will be stuck in a stagnant eddy off to the side.

Don't worry about the rocks and rapids! It's more

fun bouncing through the waves and dodging the obstacles than being stuck in a dirty, smelly pool of debris going nowhere.

I remember as a child watching a program called *Romper Room*. I used to love sitting in front of the TV performing all the actions and singing the songs. They would have a break so I'd run to the kitchen and get my cappuccino and slice of pizza (hey, I was an Italian baby!) and eat when they ate. It was Interactive Television 1970s Style!

But there was one part I didn't enjoy. It was called "Bend and Stretch". It was the exercise time. The host would say "Ready, Mr Music" then launch into the theme song: "Bend and stretch, reach for the stars."

Possibly you want to reach for the stars but aren't willing to bend and stretch. It's uncomfortable and different. It might launch you into a threatening new environment. Fear is keeping you where you feel more comfortable. Stepping out into foreign territory, learning new skills or attitudes, having to believe in yourself even more, going outside your comfort zone, feeling uncertain whether you'll make it or not—all these become reasons for putting down roots and staying right where you are.

All well and good, but you're not going anywhere. You're in a rut, and a rut is just a long grave. You'll die if you don't keep growing. So come on: start stretching! Start moving on!

Stretch Further

The world owes a lot to people who have been prepared to stretch further than anyone else.

The year was 1954. In Great Britain, a young medical student with an amazingly quick running style was in training. His dream: to become the fastest man in the world over one mile.

At the same time, the profession to which he belonged was publishing articles which supposedly proved that the human body couldn't possibly run a four minute mile. They said it wasn't able to withstand the stress, pressure or fatigue.

Roger Bannister didn't care what the "experts" said. He went out and created history. It was as if he had broken a psychological barrier because over the following two years 213 athletes emulated his feat! Today, runners looking for any kind of national or international recognition over the mile need to do it in a lot less than four minutes.

At the 1900 Olympics, Evian Bexter cleared six feet two inches at the high jump and the experts of the day said the seven foot mark was an impossible barrier. Along came a guy by the name of Fosbey who said that if athletes jumped head first and backwards they would be able to go a lot higher. Everyone ridiculed him. Fosbey ignored the critics and went away to develop this revolutionary new method, dubbed the Fosbey Flop. I wish I could have seen the faces of the so-called experts when Fosbey came out and cleared seven feet. The latest record stands at seven feet eight and three-quarter inches, and somewhere out there is a person who will break it.

If you want to be better than the best you have to be like Bannister and Fosbey and stretch further than the rest.

Stretch Beyond Pain

In my work with Youth Alive and speaking to businesspeople, I criss-cross Australia, the United States, Europe and Asia many times a year. I feel like half of my life is spent at 30,000 feet. Hand in hand with air travel goes backache, and no matter how many pillows you put behind you it seems to be impossible to prevent it.

I was complaining of lower back pain recently and made an appointment with a physiotherapist to check it out. He asked me to bend over and touch my toes, and, despite the small distance between my hands and feet, to my horror I couldn't do it.

The physio tried to extend my leg up while I was lying on my back. My whole body had tightened up. It felt like rigor mortis had set in! The physio said I had limited movement in my legs and advised me to learn to stretch, which would get rid of the back pain.

I left his office feeling dejected and sore. Then it hit

me why people go through so much pain in life and never fulfil the dreams they were meant to achieve. *They don't stretch.* They don't extend themselves beyond their pain. They limit their growth in life.

Back at the office I asked my secretary, who is also a fitness instructor, why stretching is so important. What she told me from the perspective of the physical body also relates to areas such as handling crises and developing character.

When you undergo a fitness routine, the instructor asks you to warm up and stretch first. The reason: to help your body become more flexible and supple. Why do most people lead rigid, inflexible, immovable, motionless lives? It is because they haven't stretched beyond their current achievements and dreams.

Stretching prevents injuries

I remember the first time I tried weight lifting, looking to transform myself into "Arnie" Mesiti. Being the macho man that I am, I thought, "Who needs to stretch? That's for ladies. I'm a man; I can lift these weights." A few days later there was a strong shot of pain through my shoulder, and Liz, my wife (who is a great exerciser), said, "You're crazy. You don't stretch, you don't warm up, you just get right into it."

Stretching prevents muscles from tearing and helps us flex when it feels like hell on earth. When muscles stretch they become stronger and can accomplish a lot more.

If we haven't learned to stretch ourselves we will snap when struggles and difficulties hit us. Countless people go through business troubles, financial disaster, marital breakup and other painful experiences because they haven't learned to stretch themselves to prevent injury to their business or family. You can easily see the strength of a tree in a storm by whether it snaps or is able to bend. When it splits apart it is often dry and brittle.

How is your life right now? Are you dry and brittle? Or are you flexible and supple, able to move and bend with the winds of adversity and change? Are you stretching further than before or content to stay where you are? It's not how strong the gale blows that determines your inner strength; it's your ability to withstand the pressure then come back and produce fruit. That's the strength of the tree. That's the strength of a human being.

Stretch so you can become stronger for the next level of your life.

Pat's Ten-Step Fitness Program

This is going to involve some pain. I thought I'd tell you that up-front. But it's only temporary, and when you compare the short-term discomfort of stretching with the long-term pain and agony of staying in a rut and being pushed around by crises and challenges, it's well worth it!

Here are ten straightforward steps in stretching and going beyond the average. No videos, no equipment or membership fee. Let's go!

1. Analyse.

Are you in a place of contentment, or are you longing for more, something far greater? Analyse your feelings and future desires. Be thorough: an incorrect analysis will put you on the wrong path.

Years ago I used to experience pains under my ribcage during flights, so I went to a doctor who told me I needed a gall bladder operation. I asked another doctor for a second opinion and he said the problem was a pinched nerve in my lower back. That was the correct diagnosis and it was treated. At first I was given the wrong information and it didn't relieve my pain.

If you want to get rid of the pain in your life, analyse properly, diagnose correctly, and you will get the right solution.

2. Aim.

Most people run their lives on the principle, "Ready, Fire, Aim". To move ahead you need short-term, medium and long-term aims. Start with "bite size" stretching exercises and increase them. Set your aims high, but reasonable and reachable.

3. Adjust.

If you're not heading in the direction you would ideally like to be (in relationships, income, lifestyle and so on), adjust your course. You might be busy shooting a lot of little arrows everywhere at anything. You can use the same energy to take aim with one big arrow and hit your destiny.

The story is told of a ship that was ploughing through heavy seas when it received an urgent message: "Adjust your course, you're heading in the wrong direction!" The captain replied sternly, "I am the captain of this ship. I know exactly where I am heading." The voice came back over the radio: "Adjust your course! Danger is imminent!" The captain grabbed the microphone: "I have a commission and an objective. I am heading in the direction that I need to. We are on course heading in the right direction." Back came the pleading request: "This is the lighthouse. There is an iceberg ahead of you! Adjust your course, danger is imminent!"

It takes stretching to listen to people who have a clearer picture of where we are going, and to take their advice.

4. Align.

Align yourself with people who will stretch and teach you. People who challenge your thinking, your motivation, small-mindedness and wrong perceptions. People who have been where you want to go. People who will stretch your limitations.

If a boxer only competed against easybeats he wouldn't have what it takes to become a champion. To be the best he has to fight boxers with greater ability and accept any losses as part of what will take him closer to ultimate victory.

5. Affirm.

It is important to affirm your destiny and purpose to others, to enthusiastically describe your visions, goals and dreams. Talk about where you want to go and what action you will take. This will stretch you. It will commit you to your words.

Affirmation, or self-talk, is extremely powerful. It is amazing how the mind responds when you talk to yourself. Tell it every day that you are an important person with a unique destiny and you're capable of achieving it.

6. Anticipate.

A good coach studies the opposition and anticipates their tactics. Know your opposition: the short-sighted or narrow-minded people who haven't got the courage to stretch and grow in life.

Anticipate opposition. It will come. Anticipate criticism. There will be plenty of it. If you haven't done your stretching exercises you might bow to the voices of disbelief and never discover your true purpose. As I often say to people in my talks, someone with a dream should never be at the mercy of a person who doesn't have one.

7. Apply.

Exercise seven is applying the principles of success. It isn't enough to get input and motivation from tapes, books and meetings, you have to apply what you have learned. Faith without works is dead. You may understand your profession better than anyone else, but unless you step out and "get your hands dirty" your knowledge will amount to nothing. There is an old phrase which says knowledge is power. I say knowledge without action is simply knowledge.

Knowledge is power if faith and action are applied to it.

Blondin was a tightrope walker who, to the amazement of the large crowd gathered at the top of Niagara Falls, succeeded in walking across the huge, thundering waterfall then back again. On his return the people cheered and clapped. He asked them if they believed he could do it again. They cheered louder. Then he asked if anyone would sit in a wheelbarrow and be wheeled across. The crowd was silent. Everyone believed, but no-one wanted to apply that belief.

8. Adopt.

Adopt habits that will make you stretch further. What habits do I mean? One which I began a while ago is always to have plenty of good motivational books in my briefcase. People ask how I find the time to read with my busy schedule. I make the time - whether it's between meetings, waiting for an appointment, on a bus or in a plane.

What good habits can you adopt to become more flexible?

9. Abandon.

This exercise fits in closely with the previous one. Abandon habits that will hinder your progress, such as speaking negatively, being sarcastic, telling yourself "But, I can't...", reading magazines or watching movies that drag you down emotionally.

Imagine that when you got up in the morning you didn't take your clothes off but just kept adding new trousers, shirts and coats every day. In a day or two you would feel like a space shuttle astronaut, only you'd have limited movement and be very uncomfortable (and look silly!).

Get rid of meaningless habits to create space for new good ones.

10. Accelerate

Aim higher than others' achievements - that takes a big stretch. Athletes all over the world say "That medal is mine", and each year the records get broken. Acceleration means competing against the best of the best, as well as against yourself to achieve your own best.

TAKE ACTION

The following motivators are to encourage you to keep stretching, even when it hurts.

1. What are the desires and yearnings of my heart? Is this helping me to fulfil them or get closer to them?

2. Unless I stretch, my life will stay the same. Am I willing to remain at Camp Cosy (or Fort Frustration) or do I keep moving on?

3. Stretching creates a far greater sense of fulfilment and achievement. Do I want to experience more of that?

4. There is no shortcut or quick-fix to success. Stretching further than other people want to, applying myself and working hard will help me achieve my desires. Are they worth it?

A QUICK LOOK AT STRETCHING

1. All progress is the result of stretching.

2. Stay flexible and supple.

3. Align yourself with people stretching themselves.

4. Aim higher than others' achievements.

4.
A DREAMER
LOOKS LIKE YOU

Some people find life an empty dream because they put nothing into it.

Being such an exercise junkie with a finely tuned and well proportioned body (isn't it amazing what you can get away with in a book!), I have discovered many similarities between the human body and the pursuit of your destiny. For instance, no two people are exactly alike - apart from Danny DeVito and Arnold Schwarzenegger in the movie *Twins*! We all have our own character traits, our own likes and dislikes. In the same way, all dreams and goals are unique. What excites me might bore you to tears.

The following illustration will help you to see the qualities that are needed to give you the strength of character to push forward towards your dream or to kick adversity out of the way next time it comes steamrolling into your life. Let's start at the head...

The Mind
"As a man thinks so he is" says the old proverb. In other words, you are what you think you are. "What your mind can conceive and believe you can achieve," said millionaire W. Clement Stone. That's powerful.

We can only contain one thought at a time. It's impossible to be both happy and angry. When we're facing a challenge we have a choice: decide to be either confident and positive, or depressed and full of pity. We're surrounded by negativity all day long, with language like "I can't", "I don't know how" and "I've never done it before". The winner replaces that with "I can" and "I will".

> *"Whether you think you can or think you can't, you're right."*
> **Henry Ford**

You can talk your mind into believing something. Have you ever woken up feeling less than OK and told yourself, "You're sick and need a day at home"? Or prepared for something new like a job, a driving lesson or an exam and felt the fear well up inside because of your self-talk? Forget Murphy's Law, you need Mesiti's Law:

Whatever can go right will go right because I make it right!

The Eyes

Focus and clear vision are vital. I remember as a teenager having a fight with another boy over the affections of a pretty girl. During the scuffle I looked over at her and gave a cheeky wink, as if to say "Look at me, I'm so cool"- and that's all I remember. That was the same time a fist came up and knocked me to the ground. The moral of the story is to keep your eyes on the task at hand, not just the reward.

I was distracted and I paid the price. At the same time, don't lose sight of the end result. Imagine the prize before it becomes reality. See what isn't there yet. When Youth Alive rallies barely filled a hall, I could "see" thousands of screaming kids packing auditoriums. We need to be long-sighted and visualise what we will be doing in five, ten and twenty years.

There are hundreds of young people who have told me their dream is to help other teenagers. And they will. I can see the fire in their eyes. They're hungry. They have a passion.

The Tongue
I've always got plenty to say. What I sacrifice in size I make up for in noise. Our words speak life or death, encouragement or discouragement. Choose them carefully.

When teachers, employers or managers verbally "bash" people under the guise of leadership, that's not leadership. It's assault. Former US President Dwight Eisenhower said, "I would rather persuade a man. Once he has been persuaded he will stick. If I scare him he will stay as long as he is scared and then he is gone."

Growing up in a multi-racial society was tough. You learnt at school to hit hard and run fast. We often had arguments at home and horrible things were said in the heat of the moment. They cut to the heart.

People who come from violent backgrounds don't always feel the physical pain of beatings, but they certainly remember the words that wound. People recall what you say, sometimes for years, so be an encourager. Speak words of life.

"Your tongue can destroy or build, tear up or mend. Use your words to build confidence in others."
Van Crouch

Look for things to compliment people about such as clothing, hair, appearance, manners and skills. Use words as building blocks to construct a bridge between you and the rest of the world.

The Ears

A classic example of needing the right kind of hearing occurred when I stepped off the plane at Sydney Airport after a fifty two - that's right, fifty two hour flight. I hadn't shaved or showered and had only managed a couple of hours sleep. I felt tired and irritable and just wanted to ease into a nice hot bath with a good book and an urn of Italian coffee.

Ahead of me in the terminal was an immaculately dressed woman with more diamonds than a jewellery store. She turned to me and said, "Yoo hoo, baggage boy."

My response was less than pleasant. "Lady, I'm not the baggage boy."

Liz, my wife, stopped and chastised me. She looked at me like a Mobile Conviction Unit. I hate that.

"You're the one who talks about love and accepting people. If you'd listened properly you'd have seen she is asking for help."

Don't you just hate it when they're right? I turned around with a mischievous look on my face and said, "That'll be a buck a bag, lady."

Had I listened properly I would have known that she was tired, alone and a little scared. I went back and gave her a hand.

In his book *Be A People Person*, John Maxwell recalls a comical TV sketch he once saw which shows how people hear but don't listen. It was a scenario which is probably acted out in homes all over the country:
Wife: Dear, the plumber didn't come to fix the leak behind the water heater today.

Husband (watching football game on TV): Uh-huh.

Wife: The pipe burst today and flooded the basement.

Husband: Quiet. It's third down and goal to go.

Wife: Some of the wiring got wet and almost electrocuted Fluffy.

Husband: Darn it! Touchdown.

Wife: The vet says he'll be better in a week.

Husband: Can you get me a Coke?

Wife: The plumber told me that he was happy that our pipe broke because now he can afford to go on vacation.

Husband: Aren't you listening? I said I could use a Coke!

Wife: And Stanley, I'm leaving you. The plumber and I are flying to Acapulco in the morning.

Husband: Can't you please stop all that yakking and get me a Coke? The trouble around here is that nobody ever listens to me.

Listening is a dying art in the '90s, but in order to better ourselves we need to have a sensitivity that tunes in to what people are really saying.

The Shoulders
To fulfil our dreams and weather the storms of life we need to have broad shoulders, the strength to keep on keeping on no matter what.

Do you remember the song "He Ain't Heavy, He's My Brother"? The story behind it, so I'm told, centres around a young boy who had a crippled, overweight brother. He carried that brother on his back everywhere they went. Sometimes he slipped, other times he fell over, but he never gave up.

One day a priest saw him struggling down the road and asked why he was putting himself through so much hardship.

"Son, isn't he a little heavy?"

"Sir," said the little boy, "he ain't heavy, he's my brother."

The Heart
The heart of a dreamer and overcomer is courageous and compassionate, assertive and faithful.

The Bible says, "Out of the abundance of the heart, the mouth speaks."

Your words echo your innermost feelings and attitudes.

After I'd spoken at a particular high school, one of the male students sauntered over to me. He was trying to look cool for the girls, acting really tough.

I'd been talking about what it takes to be a real man, and encouraging the girls to enjoy their femininity. He was obviously aggravated about something I had said.

He eyed me up and down and said, "I'm a man 'cause I have sex."

> *"There is something far greater than success, it is faithfulness."*
> Mother Teresa

I replied, "It takes more than having a zipper to be a man!" I hope he got the message.

Your heart dictates your actions, morals, dreams, character, family life, business life, social life - everything. Stand for something, don't fall for anything.

When you have identified your destiny, defend it, protect it and build it with courage and unending faithfulness.

Years ago, Mother Teresa was contacted by a well-meaning businessman who wanted to fly to India to give her a considerable sum of money for her work with Calcutta's beggars. But the woman who is a model of faithfulness replied, "I know you think you should make a trip to Calcutta, but I strongly advise you to save your airfare and spend it on the poor in your own country."

Sometimes it's easier to love people far away than those next door. Thousands are dying in our neighbourhoods of loneliness, rejection and hurt. The biggest disease of today is not AIDS, it's loneliness. Have a heart.

The Stomach

You are what you eat. That's almost true. If it were 100 per cent fact, I'd be a supreme pizza with olives and extra cheese!

Just as your physical body requires the right kind of energy, so does your mind.

If you have a big dream you will want to be at peak performance all your life to accomplish it. Every day I "munch" on motivational books and tapes followed by a dessert of associating with positive people and self-talk.

The Hands

You won't make it through life without hard work. Distractions, challenges and opportunities will all test you in the months and years ahead. Fight for your dream. It's yours. Don't let it get away.

Hands work. They also reach out to others. While you're focused on your future, always be ready to lend a hand to others, to offer encouragement. You reap what you sow, and from the seeds of loyalty and faithfulness will come loyalty and faithfulness. From sowing an honest work ethic and persistence will come results and success.

The Reproductive Organs

I was feeling worn out after a long week of challenging and inspiring lunchtime crowds of high school students and attending media interviews and business meetings. My body was saying, "Let's go back to the hotel room for an espresso and a long sleep." That was when a bubbly young man with a huge smile and a ton of enthusiasm came over.

"Pat, I want to be a great youth leader," he enthused.

I'd heard this before from people waiting for me to snap my fingers and turn them into a leader overnight, or those simply wanting their peers to see them talking to the guest speaker.

"So you want to be a great youth leader?"

"Yep!"

"Well, work your butt off," I replied rather abruptly.

"Thanks!" he said cheerfully, and off he went.

I thought he was a bit of a pest at the time, but later that night as I replayed the scene in my mind I realised that he was a real dreamer looking for inspiration. I didn't know how far he would get on "work your butt off".

The next time I met this jovial guy was when he asked me to speak at his youth rally eighteen months later. "Have I seen you before?" I asked.

"Yeah, you told me to work my butt off," he answered with that infectious smile. "Pat, I did exactly what you said. I started with no kids at all, worked hard and we just got 3,000 to this event!"

As you share your dreams and transfer your vision to others, some will take up the challenge to build a destiny of their own. Over the years I've reproduced Pat Mesitis all over the world with the same vision, attitude and work ethic. It's one of the great joys of being a visionary.

The Legs And Feet

Life is not a sprint race; in fact, when the walls come tumbling down and things are going crazy, it feels more like an endless marathon. But we have legs to carry us up the mountains and through the valleys, and feet to give us balance.

The secret is: don't stop! And keep everything in balance. A successful businessperson with flawed family relationships is not a success.

There's a story repeated in several motivational books about nine of the wealthiest men in the United States who met in Chicago before World War Two. They were the leaders of the steel and energy industries, the stock market and politics. Their combined assets ran into the multiplied millions (and this was back in the days when a million dollars was a big thing).

All of these great men were experts at making money, but sadly their lives were out of balance. Instead of enjoying solid family relationships, demonstrating ethical business sense and contributing to their communities, they ended their lives by committing suicide, going to jail or dying in poverty.

Good health means being healthy in every part of your body, not just your mind and feet or your heart and lungs. A stool is unstable even if one leg is just a little shorter than the others. Don't seek to excel in one area at the expense of others.

During your journey of success you will need to combine the qualities of all of the parts of the body of a dreamer. Success requires balance.

Decide to do well with self, family, marriage, friends, career, finances, community input, fitness and your spiritual "inner man".

TAKE ACTION

1. Ban "can't" from your vocabulary. Listen carefully to your choice of words.

2. List three fears in your mind.

3. List five negative inputs in your life. Determine to spend more time on positive input than negative.

4. What uplifting things can you speak out which will build others up?

5. List some ways you can reproduce yourself at work; at sports; at home.

A QUICK LOOK AT THE DREAMER IN YOU

1. You are what you think you are.

2. Focus on the prize and imagine it before it becomes reality.

3. Speak positive encouragement - "I can..."

4. Listen beyond what is being said.

5. Have the strength to keep on.

6. Have courage, compassion, faithfulness.

7. Have good input- books, tapes, videos, seminars, association with achievers.

8. Work hard.

9. Duplicate yourself.

10. Seek balance in all areas of life.

5.
SUCCESS...
IT'S YOUR CHOICE

"You get what you order in life."
A. Montapert

One of the most difficult decisions I have had to make in my life was back in 1977. I was in my late teens having just completed high school, and after much soul searching I decided on my vocation in life and filled out the application papers to go to leadership training college. It was time to tell Dad.

I remember explaining how much I wanted to give my life for something far greater than myself: people. I wanted to help young people rise up and become a generation of dreamers. He turned to me with a fierce look on his face and yelled in his Italian accent, "I putta you inna this world and I'm gonna take-a you out! Feet first!"

He wasn't very happy.

My cement shoes were ordered and the concrete was about to harden! But I had made a choice and I had to stick to it no matter what.

Dad was a peasant farmer when he migrated to Australia and he wanted the best for his kids. So he put me in the best school and worked hard so that we all had a really good chance of making it. But I didn't want to enter medical school or become an engineer as he wanted me to. It must have broken Dad's heart to see his youngest son, who was also the firstborn in his new country, receive the best education only to give it all away for a life of serving teenagers.

"God has given us two incredible things—absolutely awesome ability and freedom of choice. The tragedy is that for the most part many of us have refused them both."
Frank Donnelly

Choices aren't always easy; that one sure wasn't. But I had just exercised one of the two greatest abilities that we all have available to us. The first is the ability to make choices. The second is the ability to carry them out and fulfil our destiny in life.

Better Than Your Best

If you want to be better than you are now - better than your best - you need to make choices. The right choices. And stick to them no matter what. George Eliot once said, "The strongest principle of growth lies in human choice."

Because I work around young people so much, I get fired up when I see them grasp hold of the realisation that they choose their destinies. I get really excited when I read things like the following excerpts from a youth magazine called *Stand*, which is distributed to high schools across Australia. They confirm to me that some people in tomorrow's adult generation have woken up to the truth and are going to make major impacts on their societies.

"Who in the history of the world has ever achieved greatness or success because they just allowed life to happen to them? No-one! It's totally up to you."

"Yeah, of course, bad stuff happens to people all the time but I don't care! The buck has to stop somewhere. The most successful people are not necessarily those who come from rich families with perfect childhoods and private school educations. The most successful people are those who take hold of their own destinies."

"I've got my whole life ahead of me. Never before have I had such an unlimited amount of opportunities. And yet never before have I seen so many of our friends being ripped off because they have been sold the lie that they will never amount to anything."

Powerful!

Successful leaders in all walks of life - business, sports, politics - make a lot of choices, and stick to them. Poor leaders are slow to decide and tend to alter their decisions if the going gets tough.

> *Indecisive people are like a blind man looking in a dark room for a black cat that isn't there.*

When you make a decision regarding dreams and ambition - stick to it. Family and friends may criticise you thinking you've lost your mind. But you have a destiny to fulfil. When I look at the impact and change I've seen in hundreds of thousands of young people over the years - from South Africa to England, America to Australia, Asia and the Pacific to New Zealand - I'm glad I stuck to my decision. It has made me a far better person and made others better too. Better than our best.

My choices led to a passion, and one person with a passion is greater than ninety-nine with an interest.

Choices Decide Your Future

Unfortunately, in our soft and comfortable, what's-in-it-for-me, pleasure-seeking Western culture, we don't have to make too many decisions. The majority of people let governments and organisations do it for them.

The '90s are so vague and grey, with their compromised standards and diluted values. Society is robbing people of their independence. It would prefer that we were all "standardised" - think the same, act the same, live the same, believe the same.

But free thinking is not an option; it's a right. It requires courage to make choices. And energy. When you make a strong, committed choice you become focused on your goal. Every person who has ever achieved something (from winning a club sports event to pioneering a worldwide fast food chain) has had many, many choices, and one of them was that they wanted to succeed.

Think of the athlete who decides to compete in the Olympics and starts a chain of events that they hope will see them on the winner's dais many years in the future. Champion

"Our lives are a sum total of the choices we have made."
Dr W. Dwyer

swimmer Kieren Perkins started training for the Olympics when he was just a young boy. While his friends played with their bikes and footballs and thought about homework and girls, Kieren had an all-consuming desire to represent his country at the highest level. And he did.

And that is both good news and not-so-good news. The good news is that your choices will decide your future. The not-so-good news is that your choices will decide your future.

It's good news because if you take action and determine what you want to do and where you want to go, there's a good chance

Many people are born but they never live. And they die before they're born.

you'll get there. On the other hand, if you decide to let life take its course and allow others to make decisions for you, they will.

You didn't choose to be born. Neither did I. Our parents did that. But you can choose how to live. Each day you are faced with hundreds of big and small choices. It's up to you whether you want to take them on or ignore them.

Your Choices Affect Others
Your choices will both directly and indirectly affect other people. The choices of rock stars and Hollywood actors to live a certain lifestyle and flaunt their lack of morals and character imfluence their fans. When they choose to be self-centred and indulgent without any thought of the consequences, multiplied thousands are affected. People are impressionable and some choose to emulate their idols.

When a father decides to leave his children he has made a moral choice that will affect himself, his family, his new relationships and future generations. When businesspeople choose to use underhanded or illegal methods to speed up promotion or recognition, or to make more profits, they make a decision that will have far-reaching consequences.

How To Make A Right Choice
No doubt you want to be sure that every time you

make a decision, it's a right one. But how do you make right choices? I use this six-step checklist to help me:

1. What do I understand to be right, honourable and just?

In other words, what are my personal ethics and moral standards, and how do they weigh up against this choice I must make? Will it compromise them? Or is it in line with what I believe and live by?

2. What will the consequences be of the choice I'm about to make? Is this part of my destiny or a distraction?

This requires thinking ahead. It means analysing the effects of what I am planning to do. Will I gain? Will I lose? Will others gain too?

3. Will it help or hinder the Big Picture of my life? Will it help me get closer to my target?

Is this decision a launching pad or quicksand? Will I sink or swim?

4. How will I feel after making the choice?

It is important to consider the emotional aspects of decision-making.

Cast your mind forward to tomorrow, after you've

made your choice, and imagine how you'll feel. Confident? Proud? Ashamed? Angry?

5. How will it affect those around me? Will it launch them further to their destinies or bind them up with uncertainty and doubt?

In some cases a decision will affect more people than yourself. It will have negative or positive ramifications for your immediate family, friends, workmates or peers. Make sure you've considered them too.

6. How will I feel if someone else had to make this choice?

What advice would I give that person? You might think after going over this mental checklist that there is no ideal way of making quick, positive choices. But the more decisions you make, the easier it becomes until it is a natural process.

Wrong Choices Aren't Final
What if you make a wrong choice? Decisions can be corrected. One bad choice doesn't always have to be final.

It's like a torpedo or missile. The submarine or battleship keeps sending information to the guidance system to keep it on its path. If you find that a certain decision is wrong, make another one to correct it. It takes guts to say "I was wrong" and move across to the right track, but that is far better than saying nothing and going further and further towards a dead end.

If I cross the road to visit my neighbour and I'm off course by one degree it won't matter all that much. I'll end up in his garden or walk into a tree. But if I fly from Sydney to Los Angeles and my flight is off by one degree, who knows where I'll end up?

Back in my early days of working with young people I met a girl who was on the brink of making a terrible choice. I was talking to a group of teenagers when one of our youth workers introduced me to her. She wore pain and heartache like a heavy coat. Not only had she been through hell; she looked like she had a permanent address there.

I noted the multi-coloured hair and scars on her face and arms, and looked into the steely, cold, wounded eyes without any sparkle of life.

"Hi, I'm Pat," I said.
She didn't even give me her name. She just blurted, "I'm going to kill my father!"

I did a double take then took her aside so we could talk privately. Slowly the barriers of hate and anger came down and she began to share with me about her life. As I listened, my heart grew so heavy it felt like I had a brick in my chest. Tears filled my eyes.

This young girl was terrified of her father. Since childhood she had lived through an unspeakable tragedy of sexual, physical, emotional and verbal abuse. The scars were where he had stubbed out cigarettes on her skin. Far worse were the much deeper scars within. Not surprisingly, the roots of bitterness and revenge were deep. She had decided the only way to end her shame was to take his life.

Talking to her remains one of the most emotionally exhausting days in the eighteen years I have worked with kids.

I got Liz and certain members of our team to build a relationship with the girl and start the gradual process of healing past hurts. I kept in regular contact as well, and before long she began coming to our fun, off-the-wall youth meetings.

The months went by. We counselled, talked, cried, laughed and cried some more. She came to the point where she was able to release herself from her anger and pain, take hold of faith and hope, and start a new life. Revenge eventually turned to forgiveness.

This teenage girl had courage. She made good choice after good choice, and through it all her naturally bubbly, humorous and delightful personality sprang out. I'm happy to say that today, as a result of this perseverance and good decision-making, this once-abused teenager is a successful, bubbly chef pursuing an exciting destiny in the catering industry.

The Next Step

Choices are important, but even more important is carrying your choices out. Most people procrastinate and ponder their way to an eventual decision but don't see it through. A common example is losing weight. Critics will say, "Diets don't work: look at me." The reality is that diets do work. People don't.

Businesses work. People don't. If you've been in business for a while and still haven't seen the success you anticipated, keep at it. Keep making good choices and keep carrying them out. It's a choice.

The choices you make today determine where you will be tomorrow!

TAKE ACTION

1. What choices do you need to make that you have procrastinated over?

2. Choose the steps to help you implement those choices.

3. What are some of the hindrances you face in making choices eg. fear, insecurity, etc.

4. Develop a plan to overcome these hindrances.

5. List the areas where you have been double-minded and make a decision to be single-minded.

A QUICK LOOK AT MAKING CHOICES

1. You have two important abilities:

 • the ability to make choices

 • the ability to carry them out and fulfil your destiny.

2. Make good choices and stick to them.

3. It takes courage to make a choice.

4. Life is a series of choices.

5. If you're going off in the wrong direction, make another choice.

6. The choices you make today determine your life tomorrow.

7. The greatest waste of time, emotion and energy is indecision - it produces nothing.

6.
ALWAYS LET YOUR
CONSCIENCE BE
YOUR GUIDE

*Those who are given
to white lies soon become
colour blind.*

Remember the little character Jiminy Cricket in the Walt Disney movie *Pinnochio*? He was the puppet's conscience who told him right from wrong. Unfortunately for Pinnochio, he rarely if ever listened to Jiminy and got into a lot of trouble. One pearl of wisdom from the likeable cricket was: "Always let your conscience be your guide." That's very good advice.

A friend of mine who is a Christian minister got on a bus one day after talking to a large gathering and paid his fare. It was one dollar. Mistakenly, the driver gave him back two dollars change. His first thought was it must be a "provision from God", but then he decided to let the driver know of his error.

"Excuse me, but you've given me too much money."

"I know I did," replied the driver.

"What do you mean you knew you did?" came the bewildered response.

"I was in your meeting last night. I wanted to make sure you were the real thing."

Choices have consequences. You never know who's looking.

Decisions have a value structure and some values - such as family, marriage, trust and hard work - are not negotiable. They cannot be placed in risk. One of the things the great Indian leader Mahatma Gandhi taught was that conscience should come first and pleasure second. Pleasure without conscience is a recipe for ruin.

Choices Show Character
A few years ago I was invited to speak to people in the ghettos in New York, but I had to find the airfare because they didn't have the finances to cover it. I approached my contacts, time passed, and I hadn't yet raised the necessary funds. Suddenly, with just two weeks to go, a business-man offered to take care of everything.

I called the guys in New York (who were anxious about whether I was going to make it) and gave them the good news. They were astonished.

"Pat, I don't believe it! Most people would go out, raise five to ten times the airfare under the guise of helping the poor, then still slug us for it."

"I couldn't do that, I like to sleep at nights."

They thanked me for my honesty. And the trip was a brilliant success.

The choices you make are a reflection of your character. They reveal your inner strengths, what you're made of.

A good leader makes good choices. A corrupt leader makes corrupt choices which ultimately devastate the lives of others. Think of Hitler, Amin, Hussein.

An athlete might choose to use anabolic steroids to speed up their physical development. They are compromising good morals and ethics in exchange for possible fame and glory. From my observations, short-cuts end up becoming long-cuts and rob people of their real potential. If that athlete is drug tested they will face expulsion and disgrace, ruining all chances of being the best.

"Always tell the truth and you never have to remember what you said."
T. L. Osborn

Even small day-to-day choices must be made with integrity. An athlete needs to cut fast food, snacks, soft drink and alcohol out of their diet, go to bed on time, turn up to training whether it's cold outside or not, take their vitamins, and so on. If they don't they will never make it. It's exactly the same in the business world.

Contrast the results of bad decisions with those of making good decisions:

RESULTS OF BAD MORAL DECISIONS	RESULTS OF GOOD MORAL DECISIONS
Guilt	Guilt free
Bad reputation	Good reputation
Loss of respect	Gain respect, lead to influence
Lose trust	Trusted completely
Get caught out	Gain favour
Short-circuit future	Build future
Must have good memory for past lies	Don't need to remember
Sleepless nights	Sleep like a baby
Reproduce badness	Reproduce goodness
Reap what you sow	Reap what you sow

Dr Denis Waitley says in his book *Being Your Best* that it's a myth that the good guys finish last. He says the good guys always finish best. As a matter of fact, they're the ones who actually finish. They don't give up halfway like losers, quitters and shonks.

Top business leaders across the United States have been surveyed and most of them have strong families and are still married to their first wife. Don't believe the rumours.

Shortcuts Won't Get You Anywhere

One of the saddest cases of wrong decision-making based on the ignoring of conscience occurred on Tuesday 28 January 1986, when the NASA space shuttle Challenger blasted off.

The engineers at the launch site, Cape Canaveral, Florida, were worried about the seals on the booster rockets because of the icy weather. They voiced concerns to management that the cold could cause the seals to fail. Despite their anguished pleas, the senior officials demanded that the countdown continue. Power steamrolled reason and conscience.

Seventy seconds after lift-off the Challenger disappeared in a ball of flame as millions of gallons of fuel ignited. The seals had broken. Debris rained down over the ocean for more than an hour. Tragically, the astronauts on board endured a three and a half minute freefall in the front section of the shattered craft before hitting the sea at 200 miles per hour.

Will you be tempted to compromise in your choices? Yes. But when life seems like it has turned upside-down and there's no way out...don't lower your standards. Consider your options, and keep going. Believe that inside you is an untapped greatness. Denis Waitley calls it the "seeds of greatness". If you choose to believe you can win, and pursue success the right way, the seeds will become a fruit-bearing tree. If you don't, they will shrivel up and die.

Success is a journey through your whole life, not a single destination. It is a series of right choices.

Here's what to do. Imagine the big picture several years down the track: what you'll be doing, who you'll be with, where you'll be living, what you'll be driving, where you'll be taking your vacations. Now make long-term decisions and plans to get you there rather than shortcuts which will short-circuit your future.

I encourage you not to settle for anything less than victory in your life. The very best. Choose today to start taking small steps, the right small steps, towards that victory. The first step is deciding to take the first step. The second step is choosing never to quit.

The Right Direction
There is a powerful statement in the Bible which says that we choose life. Sadly most people choose

existence instead. Life and death, poverty and wealth, failure and success - all are in our power to choose.

Do you realise that what you choose can't be taken away from you? If you say to yourself right now that you're going to be a better person and succeed in life, and you work out the first steps to steer you in that direction, no-one can come along and say you're a failure. Their words have no affect because you've already set the wheels in motion to achieve your goal.

Dr Norman Vincent Peale was one of the greatest preachers of our century. His book *The Power of Positive Thinking* was one of the first to challenge the way we think and act. He got the theme for his ground-breaking book

Who we are today is the result of yesterday's choices. Who we will be tomorrow is the result of today's decisions.

from a verse in the Bible. It says: "Whatever things are true, are noble, are just, are pure, are lovely, of good report; if there is any virtue, anything praiseworthy, meditate on these things."

I know that the voice of doubt is shouting inside you. It's in me too. I know that people are quick to tell you, "It can't be done". I get criticised often. And I know that the Tall Poppy Syndrome causes the masses to want to drag you back to their level of mediocrity.

But the voice of destiny must be the one that shouts loudest in your heart. If at the moment it's a distant cry - decide to change it.

Protect Your Self-Worth
Negativity, despair and doubt are thrown at you by society every day. They're all around you, not just on the news at night. You need to fight negativity with positive input. Create a new self-belief. Make decisions. Have a conviction to reach your goals.

A key to making correct decisions is having a good, healthy self-image: an understanding that you are unique, important and have a destiny waiting for you. It is vital that you don't allow negative people to influence your self-worth or self-image. Not even family or close friends whom you respect.

Your brain can only focus on one thought at a time. Why not make it a positive one? Followed by another positive one. And another. And another.

Dreamers use personal attacks and difficulties as building materials for building dreams.

I use a few simple steps to keep me believing in my God-given destiny instead of what the world wants me to believe. They are:

1. Make excitement a daily habit.

2. Be excited about your future.

3. Talk about your future each day.

4. Consistently think about your future.

Most people who attack your values and dreams have none of their own. They're discouraged with life, miserable at their own lack of direction, aimless and without any purpose. They can't bear to see somebody else succeed - even someone they love - because their "failure syndrome" doesn't know how to cope with your enthusiasm and optimism.

Going back to that day when I told my family about becoming a youth leader, I'll never forget the stress I went through psyching myself up to say it and trying to explain it, then the added stress of their verbal attacks. Many things were said and done. I could have become bitter, but I didn't. It was a choice.

I survived the ordeal, and in the end my father offered to pay my training college fees. He supported me through three years of study, paid for my wedding to Liz and paid for half of our first house.

Imagine if I'd chosen to allow my Italian blood to boil, if I'd lashed back in defensiveness and insecurity, then left with a heart full of anger and bitterness. I could have destroyed our relationship forever. And it would have been a great example!

Nothing is so important that it should cause you to lose friends or rob you of your destiny.

Bitterness is like a plant. It puts down long roots which are very hard to dig out. It's all about attitudes - long-term attitudes. Attitudes that say, "I know you don't understand right now what I'm doing, but let's stay friends. I respect you for your opinions and I'd appreciate you respecting me for mine."

There's a chance that over time people will recognise what you are doing and will offer encouragement instead of antagonism. Even if they don't, you haven't allowed any friction to damage your relationships.

Three Kinds Of People
There are three kinds of people in the world: those who make things happen, those who talk about what should happen, and those who don't have a clue that anything is happening. Which one are you going to be?

The "Make It Happen" person looks like this:

They have a vision - they **SEE** it

They take action - they **DO** it

They verbalise the vision - they **TALK** it

They inspire others - they **LEAD** it

They see it happen - they **LIVE** it.

> *The two greatest days of your life were the day you were born...and the day you found out why!*

What is the "Talk About It" person like?

They have no vision, only fantastic fantasies and idealisms that lead nowhere

They're always ready to make expert comments but never do anything

They speak negatively

They are demoralising

They never see anything happen because they don't do anything and have no belief in anything.

The third category, the "I Don't Have A Clue" person, is very easy to spot:

They see nothing

They do nothing

They say nothing worthwhile

They leave nothing behind them.

I hope you've seen that choices are immensely powerful. I challenge you to choose to live in the one per cent of people bettering their best and seeking success, rather than the ninety-nine per cent who are content to wallow in compromise, mediocrity and being average. Average! Yuck! I hate that term!

Remember this anecdote:
Wishbones: wish someone else will make the choices, thus saving them the challenge of having to face their lack of progress, neutral values and under-achievement.

Jawbones: talk a lot about making choices but never get around to making them.

Knucklebones: criticise the choices made by everybody else.

Backbones: make right choices based on ethics and integrity and take action.

Become a Backbone!

TAKE ACTION

1. List the things that are non-negotiable in your life, and stick to them.

2. What are the values you most hold to in your a) family life, b) business life?

3. What are some good practical decisions you can make today that are value oriented to build a better tomorrow eg. hard work, family time, etc.?

A QUICK LOOK AT LETTING YOUR CONSCIENCE BE YOUR GUIDE

1. Decisions have a value structure.

2. Pleasure without conscience is a recipe for ruin.

3. Short-cuts end up being the long way round.

4. Don't compromise - stick to your level of integrity.

5. A healthy self-image helps in good decision-making.

PART TWO
THE JOURNEY

"The vision of things to be done may come a long time before the way of doing them becomes clear, but woe to him who distrusts the vision."
J. L. Jones

7.
20-20 VISION

*"Imagination is more
important than knowledge."*
Albert Einstein

I n my office I have a personally autographed book, *The Long Walk To Freedom*, the autobiography of Nelson Mandela. It is the story of a man who dared to have a vision for a new South Africa.

Mandela was the foster son of a Tembu chief. He grew up struggling with two worlds: the traditional culture of his tribe and the hostile reality of his white-dominated nation. His passion and vision grew out of the horrors and atrocities that were happening to his countrymen. Armed with fierce determination, he set a course to break down apartheid, and this led to a life in prison. But more than twenty years behind bars didn't stop his vision, and the world looked on in awe as this man made the progression from prison to presidency.

One of the imperatives for success in life is vision. People with vision, ideas, creative gifts, innovativeness and talents - people who develop channels in their lives for these abilities - achieve success. Those who are creative with their visions are also the ones who attract others to them. Vision has to be creative, different and inspiring.

> *"Don't let anybody steal your dream."*
> *Dexter Yager*

Ray Kroc sold paper cups to restaurants in the 1920s and worked his way up to become a top salesman. But his vision went way beyond paper cups. He dreamed of making a big impact on the restaurant business, so he quit sales to market a machine that could mix several milkshakes at a time. When you have a dream opportunities come to you. Through promoting the milkshake machines he met the McDonald brothers, who ran a highly successful restaurant. They got talking and Ray Kroc ended up becoming their partner.

Driven by his vision he came up with the concept of duplicating the McDonalds' restaurant on the other side of town. The two brothers opposed this, so Kroc bought the restaurant from them. Back at a time when hamburgers and chips were not an accepted meal, the pioneer began developing his empire. For the first eight years he poured all he had into the concept and saw few profits in return. But today, by comparison, I read that in the first three months of 1989 his family estate received $189 million!

Ray Kroc had a vision and he changed the world.

Walt Disney did the same. He had to approach 303 banks before he could find one willing to finance his wild, crazy scheme to put a fun park with a cartoon mouse in a swamp area.

Neil Armstrong, the first man to walk on the moon, said that ever since he was a boy he'd had a dream of doing something important in aviation.

"If you can dream it, you can do it. Always remember this whole thing was started by a mouse."
Walt Disney

"Dreams are our first casualty in life," says Kevin Costner, one of the most applauded actors of our time. "People seem to give them up for 'reality'."

Vision Breeds Success

In my work with youth I have discovered that one of the things young people love is vision and challenge. It's funny watching them at youth camps, especially the guys trying to show off their macho abilities. They'll do anything to attract a girl.

There was one occasion when a guy climbed onto rocks and performed a Tarzan-like dive into the water far below in order to attract the attention of a group of girls. He gave no thought to what might be under the water, he just jumped. He ended up breaking his collarbone and arm. When I visited him in hospital, the first thing he said was, "Pat, did they see what I did?" His vision wasn't to perform an awesome dive so much as to be a hit with the girls.

To be a successful person, regardless of your age, you must have a vision of where you want to be. Vision will cause you to be stretched far beyond the abilities you currently possess. It will launch you into abilities you don't have right now.

Will there be pain along the way? You bet. But betterment by its very nature is about vision, and being a better person is worth the pain it takes to get there.

An athlete has a vision for gold. A businessperson has a vision for success and profits. A mother has a vision for bringing up well-balanced children in a happy family. What is your vision for life?

In the book *Vision, Values and Courage*, Neil Snider, James Dowd and Diane Morse-Houghton say: "Vision must provide a clear image of a desirable future. One that represents an achievable, challenging and worthwhile long range target."

Vision isn't a goal. It's a picture, a canvas on which you paint your future. It shows you what the future could and should look like. The businessperson's canvas shows them standing in front of a tall modern building with their company name on it - a sign of their success. The athlete's painting shows them standing on the dais holding up the gold medal, surrounded by cheering fans. And a young man wanting to win the heart of his sweetheart envisions himself at the altar with his beautiful bride.

Leaders Have Vision

Those of us in leadership have a painting of where we are going and we are transforming it into living reality to affect the lives of people around us. The wonderful thing about vision is that it is not something you manage but something you lead people in to. I have seen companies, organisations and churches being managed, not led. The reason why they aren't led is because there is no vision.

To be better than yourself and a great leader, you need to lead people to a goal worth achieving. The vision creates inspiration, which leads to perspiration (and more than a little frustration). With a vision a team of workers become more than just workers - they become an army. It is a rallying point. It gives them meaning and purpose.

Communication and personal example are of the utmost importance in passing on vision. Here's a simple but powerful strategy I use when transferring vision to my colleagues:

1. Keep it simple.

A cluttered or hazy vision doesn't give people an accurate picture of where they are going.

2. Stick to the core issues.

These are what is important. At Youth Alive, the core issue is to reach young people. However, how we do it is as creative and diverse as you can imagine. When speaking to corporations, the core issue is to motivate people to a life of excellence. How we do it varies greatly, from speaking to video, drama or pictures. But the core issue is to motivate.

3. Repeat it before people.

People need to be constantly reminded and motivated. Repetition is one of the greatest tools of teaching—ask any teacher. How many times at school did you do your two times table?

4. Stress its importance.

People start to "own" the vision as they catch your enthusiasm, passion and drive.

5. Show people how to attain the vision.

I hear a lot about delegation, but unless people have mastered a task or have a good understanding of how you want it done, how can they be delegated to do it with accuracy and intelligence? Show them how.

6. Help them attain it.

A baby needs to be helped to take its first steps. A child needs assistance to ride a bike for the first time. By helping them, you lead them towards fulfilling their own vision.

7. Show them the consequences of reward and failure.

Build their motivation to succeed.

8. Celebrate the small victories.

Each small celebration inspires people on to the next one. This is one of the reasons I enjoy speaking at big functions like Amway business seminars. They celebrate each small victory that leads up to the prestigious Diamond level.

Every achiever, whether at a high or low level, is applauded.

9. Make sure each team member is aware of how their personal input is contributing to corporate success.

People need to know that their contribution has meaning and is appreciated. This gives them a sense of ownership of the vision and inspires them to greater achievements.

This doesn't mean you can't be flexible; it means you set a standard and stick to it.

*Turn your present into a vision
of how you want the future to be.*

Vision Creates The Future
Commitment to vision is an awesome power. If you decide to persistently move towards your goal over days, weeks, months or even years you will change your life, the lives of people around you, and your world. Regardless of setbacks.

Have you ever seen a successful athlete suffer injury and then come back to win the prize...a failed businessperson start all over again from zero and become a huge success...a husband and wife come back from a failed marriage to build a solid, secure family unit? It is because the vision stayed alive despite their circumstances.

If you have a vision it eases the pain when you face problems. They lose some of their sting. The vision lifts you above the difficulties and gives you strength to persevere through them and out the other side.

You can change the way you think about your work, your employer, the people who work for you, and your future. It's a decision.

TAKE ACTION

1. What picture (vision) do you have of your future? Write it here:

Career

Family

Home

Lifestyle

Car

Travel

Other

2. How will you reach it?

3. JUST DO IT!

A QUICK LOOK AT VISION

1. A vision is vital for success in your life.

2. Vision stretches you beyond your current abilities.

3. Vision provides direction.

4. Vision creates inspiration.

5. Know your vision in detail, repeat it daily.

6. Show others how to reach the vision.

8.
DEFINING YOUR DESTINY

"My mamma always said 'I happen to believe you make your own destiny. You have to do the best with what God gave you'."
Forrest Gump, from the movie Forrest Gump

C ontemplate these extremely profound and powerful thoughts from a fired-up eighteen year old, Bec Woof, in an article which appeared in the youth magazine *Stand* in my home town.

"The Oxford Dictionary defines destiny as the predetermined events of a person's life. The word is derived from destination - the place where a person or thing is bound. Fate, by definition, is virtually the same as destiny, being 'power predetermining events from eternity'. There is a difference though. Fate conjures up a sense of inevitability and passivity, where life just happens to you, where you are the victim. Basically, it means you've got no control whatsoever over your circumstances.

"Destiny, however, is positive. It means that you have an active role to play in making your life happen. Life is what you make it. Take ahold of what's yours and go for it! Take every opportunity by the teeth and milk it for all it's worth. Some doors only open once. Every day, every decision we make takes us either one step closer or one step further away from our potential. Where are you headed?!" It fires me up when I see our nation's young people grasping the reality of vision and destiny.

Boredom is not a result of having nothing to do but of having nothing to live for.

One young man I met had an outstanding future. He was intelligent, handsome, funny, the one you would have nominated *"Most Likely To Succeed"*. But he was bored and through this lack of direction he became entangled in a web of drugs. Soft drugs led to heroin and before long he had put so much of it into his arms that he had nowhere else to inject it.

One day he went to his parents, who loved him dearly, and said, "If you get me a brand new motorcycle I won't be bored any more and won't need to do drugs." Thinking they were doing the right thing, they bought him a brand new Ducati, a beautiful piece of Italian engineering, and he decided to go "cold turkey".

I don't know if you've ever seen a junkie go through detoxification, or the DTs. They suffer shakes, hot and cold sweats, cramps and headaches. It's day after day of agony. They scream for the next fix. It's a very ugly sight.

The thrill of the new Duke only lasted a few days and the young man was bored again. The cramps and sweats were too much, so he went back to the dealer for another fix. The price was high - he had to exchange the bike to purchase some "good stuff". Tragically, he was sold heroin mixed with battery acid and it killed him.

I got the phone call at one o'clock that morning. It was his distressed mother. "He's dead! Pat, he's dead!"

I dressed quickly and raced to the hospital. I hate losing one of "my boys" - especially to something as senseless and destructive as drugs. He was lying on a trolley ready to be wheeled away to the morgue. His head was swollen, his face was twisted in pain and his arms were covered in horrible veins and scabs from the hundreds of injections. What a pathetic sight. Another destiny had disappeared.

It wasn't drugs that killed this young man. It was a lack of purpose. He had nothing to live for.

His parents asked me to conduct the funeral and it was a grey day when we stood around the graveside watching the casket lowered into the ground. I listened to the sobs of a distraught mother, closed my notes, and stared firmly at the group of people from the drug world who had come to pay their last respects.

"That's your destiny!" I stated. You should have seen the looks on their faces. It wasn't a time for pretty words. I began to challenge them.

"When you pass on to eternity, live so the preacher won't have to lie at your funeral. Drugs don't make you popular, cool or sociable. They make you dead. Your destiny is too important to waste!"

Lack of direction is a huge dream killer. It rips you off, steals your destiny. You must have life goals. You must know where you're going, otherwise the next time you feel like you're on a scenic tour of hell you'll end up booking in and staying there.

Get direction. Get vision. It has a protective power. It has explosive power. And it gives you staying power.

In his book *Strategy For Daily Living*, Ari Kiev of Cornell University says: "In my practice as a psychiatrist I found that helping people to develop personal goals has proved to be the most effective way to help them cope with problems. Observing the life of people who have mastered adversity, I have noticed that they have established goals and fought with all their effort to achieve them."

Discover Your Destiny
First of all, destiny is not Pollyanna, fairyland, misguided, hyped-up, air-headed ra-ra. It is a positive, calculated belief in your own destiny.

Knowing your life purpose will take time. In fact, it is an ongoing thing. You will come to understand it better as you journey further and further along that four wheel drive road of life.

Having a destiny will help you put your thoughts in order. It will make it easier to sort out priorities.

When I was young I dreamed of being a singer. If you've heard me sing you'll know it sounds something like Rod Stewart in a blender. I was driving along with my wife one day when

"Have a definite clear goal and objective."
Aristotle

the Michael Bolton song *"How Am I Supposed To Live Without You"* came on. I started singing along with Mike,

"How am I supposed to live..."

Liz interrupted,

"Keep that up and you'll find out."

My next childhood dream was to be a teacher. Interestingly enough, I now spend a lot of my time standing in front of young people in school halls, church halls, even condemned halls, teaching them. But my messages aren't calculus, modern literature or economics; they're success principles for life.

While I was building up Youth Alive I developed a deep desire to inspire and encourage businesspeople. It's amazing how destinies collide.

I was in a lift in a hotel thousands of kilometres from home when I met a successful network marketer. He had heard a little of my work with young people and he asked me to speak at a function. I thought,

"What's a function?"

I went along to that event not really knowing who would be there or how they would respond to my message.

From that chance meeting came a whole new direction which now sees me addressing businessowners all over Australia, New Zealand and the United States.

It's not coincidence, it's destiny.

Make A List
Perhaps you've never defined your destiny before now. You will need to put time aside and get away from the speed and activity of everyday life.

Find a quiet corner, take a pen and notepaper, and think about what is really important to you. Happiness? A loving family? Enough income not to worry about the bills? Working with kids? Completing a degree? Becoming a leader in your field of expertise? Mastering a new skill? Being a friend to the lonely? Buying a new car?

Before long you will have a list. Possibly you are seeing for the first time the very things you have been carrying in your heart all these years.

You could place your dreams in categories such as Self, Family, Community, Financial, Work, Recreation, Spiritual.

Now write down your desires, dreams and needs in these different areas of life. For example, I had a dream to hold the biggest youth rallies in Sydney, attracting over 40,000 people. I couldn't achieve it in a month, or even in a year, so I had to list it in the future.

In front of that dream of mine came a string of goals which would have to be achieved first so that the ultimate dream could become reality.

From this list I looked at what had to be done today, this week, next week, this month, next month, over the next six months, the next twelve months, the next two years and the next five years.

By doing this I determined the route to my future. It gave me huge belief that I would make it.

As a matter of interest, I wrote the step-by-step goals in pencil because I am aware that sometimes, especially when crises strike, we have to modify them in order to stay on course.

I saw that in order to reach some steps I would need to include someone else, or learn a new skill. Knowing this well in advance prepared me. Obviously, one person could not oversee the whole Youth Alive movement. As I have progressed closer to my ultimate desires, I have had to include people with managerial, secretarial, organisational and technical skills.

Another habit I have picked up from reading motivational books is to collect photos of my dreams. I read a lot, taking notes, and put pictures up on the wall to keep the visual image in front of me.

The mind cannot differentiate between perception and reality.

Get Emotional

I remember years ago standing in the biggest entertainment venue in Sydney and "seeing" it filled with excited young people, the air full of anticipation, an incredible light show and a top band of professional musicians onstage. That was while I was working long hours organising rallies for just 1,000 people.

The auditorium was dark and empty - lifeless. Yet in my mind a wide-screen video was playing with colour and noise and action. I had no idea how long it would take to reach my dream. I just believed if I kept doing what I was doing and imparted that vision to my team it would come to pass. And it did.

All of the books I have read about dream-building and goal-setting say that it is vital to emotionalise what you want. Drive that car, put on that dress, walk through that display home, sit in that chair. Not just once, but as often as you can. Remember how it looks, the smells, the feeling of anticipation, the quickening of your pulse as you touch it. Get the brochure or the fabric swatch. Look at it every day. Talk about what life will be like when you have it.

What you are doing is setting up a belief that you will achieve your goals. You are becoming single-minded. Focussed. The mind cannot differentiate between perception and reality, so it begins to work out how you are going to reach that destination. And, when you're fired with enthusiasm by your dream, you won't stop next time you're going through a crisis!

Destiny, as eighteen year old Bec Woof sees so clearly, doesn't just happen. Don't wait around for it to fall into your lap. Go out and find it!

TAKE ACTION

1. What is your heart's desire for your business? For your family? Marriage? Friends? Community involvement? Changing your world? (In no more than three sentences each.)

2. What practical steps can you take in each of these areas to reach those levels of desire?

- Today

- This week

- This month

A QUICK LOOK AT DEFINING YOUR DESTINY

1. Lack of direction leads to boredom.

2. Lack of direction is a dream killer.

3. Having goals helps to solve problems in life.

4. Knowing your destiny is an ongoing process.

5. Write lists of the things you want to do/ have/achieve/learn. Prioritise them and give them deadlines. Work out the steps to reach them.

9.
SACRIFICE AND DISCIPLINE
(THE "YUCK!" WORDS)

"Only the man who can impose discipline on himself is fit to discipline others."
William Feather

Sacrifice. Discipline. Commitment. Perseverance. Faithfulness. Loyalty. Delayed gratification.

Feeling nauseous yet? These words conjure up mental images of pain, agony and years of frustration in search of a dream. They're becoming less and less popular, especially to the Leisure-Pleasure Generation of today.

But I'm here to tell you that conquering challenges, pursuing dreams and emerging from trials and tribulations stronger and wiser than before involves all of these qualities.

Every successful person I have met in business, sport or the church world has had to make sacrifices.

> *Success has a high price, and so does failure. But failure will cost you more.*

I love speaking to network marketing groups. People often take cheap shots at these wonderful dreamers, claiming they're in get-rich-quick schemes. This is nothing but a total lie and an indication of their ignorance. I don't know anyone who promotes that philosophy. What I see is the spirit of sacrifice evident in those people - sacrificing relaxation time, sleep time, finances and effort, and being open to criticism and disappointment in order to become successful. Some of these networkers have told me how they are criticised for spending too much time showing their business plans and being out with people, yet the critics fail to realise that all successful people work late nights and pay the price.

The Missing Ingredient

Sacrifice is missing from our world today. In my first few years in youth work, I lived in a run-down house which leaked so much that when it rained the water came up to my ankles! I drove a beat-up old car, spoke at distant country towns nobody else wanted to go to, wrote articles for magazines that nobody else cared to support, spent money on petrol and oil and tyres.

For our first youth seminar we had to save up so we could do our research and buy the books they needed. I paid the price for years. Today I don't have a clunker of a car or a leaking home. The going-without has paid off.

People love the fruits of success,
but forget the roots of success

There are no shortcuts. If you want to get to the top of the ladder, start at the bottom. Accept the sacrifices, pay the necessary debts and you will reap incredible rewards.

The athlete controls his food cravings when friends indulge. He goes to bed at certain times while friends are out socialising. He trains early every day while they take it easy or sleep in. But it's all worthwhile when weighed up against the ultimate prize: the gold medal.

Any success without pain is short-lived. As the preacher Robert Schuller says, "No pain, no gain."

Proverbs 20:21 tells us that an inheritance gained quickly at the beginning will not be blessed at the end. That's why many people who win lotteries waste their riches. Some end up with less than they started with because they didn't know the value of a dollar.

"I've never known a man worth his salt who in the long run deep down in his heart didn't appreciate the grind, the discipline."
Vince Lombardi

This subject makes me think of the businesspeople I speak to. A major part of their businesses involves personal development programs which teach them over a period of time how to control wealth and use it properly. By the time they are making a lot of money, they have a clear understanding of how to ensure money is their servant, not their master. I see them making very wise financial decisions.

If you can learn to be faithful with a little, you will more than likely be able to handle the bigger things later on.

Persevere At Persevering
Author Ted Engstrom says, "Rewards for those who persevere far exceed the pain before victory." Benjamin Franklin said, "The things which hurt instruct." And Samuel Johnson said, "Great works are performed by perseverance."

Perseverance and sacrifice go hand in hand. In his brilliant book *Empires of the Mind*, Denis Waitley says there are six areas which are necessary for us to move ahead:

1. Sacrifice and discipline.

2.Controlling thoughts and imagination and channelling them properly.

3. Controlling our attitudes, staying positive.

4. Controlling our tongues, the words we say and tones we use.

5. Controlling the promises we make, becoming reliable.

6. Controlling our responses to things we have no control over.

All of these involve sacrifice and perseverance.

Self-discipline makes you the disciple. You become your own trainer, your own coach, your own teacher and disciplinarian. This is far too hard for many people in the soft '90s, but it is essential for success.

Sacrifice can be as simple as deciding to switch off the Idiot Box, which robs you of valuable hours each day, so you can enjoy more quality time with your family. Or playing golf every second weekend instead of every week. Uncomfortable changes, but changes which are necessary.

Sacrifice is required to be a team player in your department at work or on the sporting field.

Would you rather be an outstanding individual on an average team, or a member of an outstanding team? There's no room for prima donnas when you're working together.

The ability to succeed in spite of your failures in the past also involves sacrifice. It means saying to yourself, "I will not quit."

Uncomfortable? Most likely. Necessary? Definitely.

Sacrifice Pays Great Rewards

I hope you aren't about to put this book down and say: "It's too hard. Self-discipline is too painful. Sacrifice is more than I can take. I've got enough crises happening now in my life without making things tougher."

Let me remind you that sacrifice pays a great reward.

When students receive their diplomas on graduation day, the years of study and research become a distant blur. The absolute joy is worth it.

When athletes stretch to the limit and beat their previous best times you can see the happiness all over their faces.

When business-owners have the best ever year and break all the profit records, they forget the leaner years.

Every victory adds to your testimony.

A veteran black preacher from the Deep South of America once stared over his pulpit at the group of ministry college students in his congregation one Sunday. "At the end of your life," he thundered, "you will be known as someone with a title or a testimony.

Pharaoh had a title. Moses had a testimony. Nebuchadnezzar had a title: King of Babylon. Daniel and the three Hebrew boys had a testimony: out of the fiery furnace."

> *We can decide to play now and pay later, or pay now and play later.*

Testimony - which is the a c c o m p l i s h m e n t , breakthrough, success as a result of sacrifice and determination - will always be greater than a title or letters after your name. Titles are given but a testimony is earned. You might not be a Sir or Lady, but a commitment to achievement will create a testimony as impressive, if not better, than theirs.

It's Worth It!
My work takes me away from home a lot. It's an emotional, physical and mental strain. When people ask me where I live, I reply "Qantas!" It's a big sacrifice, a real cost. But the rewards outweigh the cost.

My office receives many letters from young people with testimonies of change and joy. Just last week I read a letter from a man in prison. He had wanted to kill himself, but now, due to the time I'd spent with him, he can't wait to get out and make something of his life.

What joy! What freedom!

I got another note from a young girl who was molested for twelve years. She came to us broken and hurting. Today she is a prosperous lady full of vision and hope. It's all worth it.

One letter was from a young man who came to one of our motivational seminars. I could sense the emotion in his words. It was a heartbreaking story.

He had gone away for the weekend to learn more about developing himself and reaching his destiny. He flew home. His wife picked him up at the airport and was unusually quiet all the way home. As they drove up to the front gate she gave him the news: "I'm leaving you."

He told us that what we shared at the seminar gave him the strength to cope in the midst of confusion and pain. He was able to find peace, encouragement and resilience in one of the darkest periods of his life.

He didn't have the answers and the crisis was far from over, but he had learned that you don't stop. Keep pressing forward.

When convicted criminals find the motivation to begin life over again, it's worth it.

When disenchanted young people become fine members of society and bring significant change to their community, it's worth it.

When broken men and women facing the tragedies and crises of life find the strength to not give up, it's worth it. The sweet victory of sacrifice tastes a lot better than the bitterness of failure.

Taste and see!

TAKE ACTION

1. What areas in your life need discipline?

2. List 5 time wasters.
-
-
-
-
-

3. Make it an aim to start NOW to stop the lack of discipline in your life.

A QUICK LOOK AT SACRIFICE AND DISCIPLINE

1. Sacrifice, discipline, commitment and perseverance are vital to those who want to fulfil dreams and overcome challenges and crises.

2. All successful people make sacrifices.

3. There are no short cuts. If you want to get to the top, start at the bottom.

4. Wealth gained quickly is wasted.

5. Control your thoughts and speech.

10.
AM I HAVING FUN YET?

*If you're not living on the edge
you're taking up too much space!*

My friend's speed boat bounced through the choppy waves. I stood in the cabin in a wetsuit looking something like Batman's arch enemy, the Penguin, without the beak. It highlighted all the bumps in my body, like my little buddha belly.

I looked across the bay at the constant activity. All around us people were diving off yachts, being towed on wave runners and sea biscuits, laughing and having a lot of fun. I watched the small boards skim over the waves at speed, their riders being flicked from side to side.

"I wish I could do that," I thought, "But I can't swim."

A battle was being fought in my mind. In the red corner: the Adventurous Spirit. In the blue corner: Mr Fear. Round one. The Adventurous Spirit came out strong with a blow to the left, another to the right, but back came Mr Fear with an illegal kidney punch. Adventurous Spirit staggered back. Wham!

Uppercut. Down he went. Mr Fear strutted around the ring...

"Man, I'd love to do that, but I can't swim."

Look out behind you! Adventurous Spirit got up off the mat, winding up for a haymaker. Whack! Mr Fear hit the canvas with a thump. One, two, three, four. All of a sudden I decided to try something for the first time. I put on a life jacket and thought, "At least I can float around if I fall off." I hopped on the sea biscuit behind my friend's boat and he hit the throttle. Faster and faster, with me bouncing everywhere.

Let me tell you how much I bounced. I bounced around so much that I couldn't sit down for days. My little body looked like a rubber ball on concrete. My head went one way, my legs went the other way, and my body tried to keep all of me connected. But with every bounce came a humungous laugh from deep within me. I was really enjoying myself. It was fun. (The only problem was that, because I laughed so much, I swallowed gallons of water. That was the un-fun part. Green is not my favourite skin colour.)

At the end of the high speed adventure I lay on the deck totally exhausted, feeling sick as a dog, sore all over, but absolutely content because I had done something for the first time.

The quickest cure for doubt, indecision or indifference is adventure and attitude. An attitude that says "I am destined for greatness" opens the door to personal disci-

> *A sense of adventure is needed for a life of excellence.*

pline, patience, integrity, courage, faith, humility, humour, confidence, bridge-building, love and charity.

It's Not Fun Any More
I've seen a number of people involved in youth work, counselling, the ministry and business life go through the phenomenon psychologists call "burn out".

I often say to my team that I have no time for burn out. I'm too busy having fun.

Burnout comes from having an unbalanced life.

Top corporate executives have been known to "run out of steam" after spending years working 100 hour weeks and handling huge responsibilities. There wasn't any discipline in their lives.

They went without family time, recreation time or time alone. With imbalance came a huge stress attack.

What's a good cure? Taking chances (like bouncing along behind a speedboat at 100 kilometres an hour!), being adventurous and keeping a positive attitude.

Adversity, when life had lost its sparkle, brings out the best in great leaders.

How many famous people have affected the way we live today because their attitude was bigger than their handicap?

Take away the use of his legs and you have Sir Walter Raleigh. Deafen a maestro composer and you have Beethoven. Lock him in jail and you have author John Bunyan. Condemn him with religious persecution and oppression and you have the great Christian reformer Martin Luther. Put her in one of the most poverty-stricken and violent places on earth and you have the aging Mother Teresa.

Take away her hearing and speech and you have Helen Keller. Unjustly persecute and imprison him for much of his life and you have Nelson Mandela. Accuse him of being retarded and unteachable and you have Albert Einstein. Afflict him with infantile paralysis and confine him to a wheelchair and you have Franklin D. Roosevelt. Oppress him with racial discrimination and injustice and you have Martin Luther King.

Every one of these famous people had to fight against great odds. Success was not handed out to them, they had to fight for it. And fight hard. And in every instance there was a common key: attitude.

Raleigh wrote *History of the World* during a thirteen-year imprisonment. Bunyan penned *Pilgrim's Progress* from his cell. *Robinson Crusoe* was created in jail. Luther translated the Bible for the common man while confined to a castle. Dante, the author of *The Divine Comedy*, worked in exile under the sentence of death. Einstein defied his critics and became a celebrated genius. Beethoven's most renowned compositions came when he was almost totally deaf. Luther King defied the odds and stood against the white status quo. And Mandela holds the highest office in his nation and has helped to smash apartheid.

> *"Great men are meteors designed to burn so the earth may be lighted."*
> **Napoleon**

The thing that made these people different was attitude and an adventurous spirit despite their circumstances.

In the words of author J. Sidlow-Baxter: "What is the difference between an obstacle and an opportunity? Our attitude toward it. Every opportunity has difficulty and every difficulty has an opportunity."

As Napoleon put it, "Impossible is a word to be found only in the dictionary of fools."

TAKE ACTION

1. List five activities you cannot see yourself doing but would love to do.

2. What is something you've always wanted to do but haven't as yet?

3. What plans have you made to achieve it?

4. Are you making progress or is it time to reset your plans?

A QUICK LOOK AT HAVING AN ADVENTUROUS SPIRIT

1. A sense of adventure creates a life of excitement and excellence.

2. A sense of adventure is a quick cure for doubt or indecision.

3. A sense of adventure is healthy. It adds fun to your life and reduces harmful stress.

4. Adversity brings out the best in leaders.

11.
BECOME A RISK TAKER

Abandonment: to yield to an unrestrained impulse.

I've been asked the question a thousand times; I guess it's only to be expected when I speak to at least 300,000 people (including 100,000 high school kids) every year. "What do you consider to be one of the problems facing people today?"

The person asking always expects me to say rebellion, drugs, free sex or materialism. They are often surprised when I reply, "The major problem facing people today is that they have no conviction or passion in life."

Convictions are what give you purpose, something to live for, an aim in life. Think of the generations that have gone to war with conviction in their heart; they have sacrificed everything for what they believe.

I think of the stories I've read of mild-mannered people who became heroes in combat or rescue situations because of their inner conviction.

People choose their preferences but die for their convictions.

There was the small boy who smashed through thick ice with a tree branch - a feat most adults would find difficult - to rescue a drowning mate. The mother who lifted up a car to save a child pinned underneath. The marathon runners who put their bodies through the most excruciating pain, and then, despite total exhaustion, sprint the final hundred metres to the line.

That inner rush, that inner push, that inner drive, whatever you want to call it, is much more than a second wind. It is a sense of abandonment. Abandonment to the cause, to the price, to the finish line. The spirit of abandonment.

I looked up abandonment in a dictionary and here's what I found: "To relinquish oneself, to yield to an unrestrained impulse." That is what is missing in today's generation.

Now Or Never
When was the last time you had an "unrestrained impulse" to achieve something? To go for it regardless of the odds? Are you yielding to the exciting spirit of "now is the best time to start", of "now or never"? Or are you holding back?

The best time to start pursuing your destiny is now! The best time to shake off your miseries and take the first step is today!

Sadly, many people believe in procrastination rather than progress. "Tomorrow is a good time to start. I'll get ready today and start on it in the morning." But tomorrow never comes. How do I know? I've been there.

The '90s can be for you a time of yielding to the dreams and destiny of your life. Of grasping hold of an exhilarating spirit of abandonment. Of becoming a risk taker. The difference between a wishful thinker and an achiever is risk. One person thinks about the future, the other one chases after it.

Where does the spirit of abandonment come from? It is the result of a personal conviction that you are important and you have a direction in your life, and that this cause far outweighs the struggle, fears and pain. It's based on "founded hope" - that's hope that is not pie-in-the-sky but built on a foundation of dreams, work and destiny.

I plan to speak at certain events around the world and write great books. These are part of my dream, my destiny. They're not wishful thinking. I believe they will come true and I'm pursuing those opportunities with unrestrained impulse.

As we were about to embark on a major project called Wonderfest, one of the largest youth music festivals ever held in Australia, a good friend of mine commented, "Pat, you take some big risks." Wonderfest had a budget of half a million dollars.

We were already feeling financial pressure from our other rallies and projects, but I just knew I had to do it. I had a drive in me to make Wonderfest a reality. So the team and I attacked it with a wonderful spirit of abandonment - no wishful thinkers there - and the outcome was mind-blowing! Lives were changed, broken hearts were healed, and the kids enjoyed themselves in a drug and alcohol-free environment. It was worth it. This three-day music festival is still talked about, but it would never have become a reality if we hadn't abandoned ourselves to do it.

Avoid Risk, Avoid Living
Life is risky. Love is risky. Success is risky. To avoid risk is to avoid living.

To marry is a risk. Will our relationship grow and last? To have children is a risk. Will they be ugly or good looking like their parents? To go to university is a risk. Many people drop out before graduation.

To cross the road is risky. So is flying. To have faith in something or someone is risky. I believe in a loving God who created you and me. That belief brings a lot of ridicule and sarcastic comments, but it doesn't matter.

> *Someone with a belief is never at the*
> *mercy of a person without one.*

When people say "I could never do that" they have

just cut off their future. They are trapped in today. How terrible! Don't go looking for an easy road. The highway of life is littered with aimless, sleepy "drivers"

To face risks with unrestrained impulse is to live a quality life.

going nowhere fast. Break free with abandonment.

Going The Extra Mile

There's no better way to explain abandonment than by the principle of "going the extra mile". Maybe you're familiar with the teaching of Jesus to walk two miles with someone when they ask you to walk one, or to turn the other cheek if someone strikes you, or to give them your shirt and coat when they only ask for your shirt. All of this illustrates the spirit of abandonment.

If a person were to hit you, you would probably consider two options: hit them back or walk away and do nothing. When I was at high school I always went for the first, and I made sure they hurt a lot worse than I did.

Abandonment introduces a third choice: turn the other cheek and go the extra mile. That involves a certain amount of risk and takes courage. You go beyond what is reasonable, beyond what is expected of you. And that's how we tell the difference between good people and great people.

The heroes of life are totally unreasonable in their commitment, faith and determination. Was Martin Luther King reasonable? No way. Nelson Mandela? Definitely not. They went the extra mile.

What is the biggest obstacle to having this "dare to dream" attitude? Fear. Fear of the unknown, of failing, of loss of reputation (what will your friends say?). Fear is cruel and ugly. It stifles and paralyses, cripples and oppresses. If there is fear in your heart the spirit of abandonment does just that...it abandons you.

> *Someone has defined fear as "False Evidence Appearing Real"*

Courage conquers fear. Courage means stepping out despite the way you feel. The butterflies are still flapping around inside your gut, your palms are still sweaty, but you're taking a risk anyway.

Because I Want To

Ask yourself: Is the dream and destiny for your life a conviction or merely a preference? Something you'll fight for or something you'll give away as you settle for second-best?

Is it imperative that you graduate, make the team, win the event, get the promotion, set up your own business, or have a family? Will you struggle for your dreams? To be certain, check the following comparisons between preference and conviction.

WHEN SOMETHING IS A PREFERENCE YOU:

- do things because you have to

- do things when you feel like doing them

- regard it simply as an option you can take

- change it if it becomes too difficult

- are open to changing your opinion and taking an opposite stance

- fail to give it a clear definition

- fail to reach it

- go nowhere and are unable to lead people anywhere

WHEN SOMETHING IS A CONVICTION YOU:

- do things because you want to

- do things whether you feel like it or not

- do things out of compulsion

- keep it fixed and unchanged

- seal it in your heart with unwavering belief

- make it attainable, measurable and of value

- pursue it to the end

- become a leader of others looking for someone going somewhere

Are you convinced that you are in the right business - or just a business? Are you loyal to your employer or employees? Do you have a conviction that yours is the best product? The best business system? The best support structure? Conviction knows the answer to such questions; preference doesn't.

Australia has the shameful statistic of one in three marriages failing. This is because marriage is regarded as preference, not conviction. A man prefers his wife for the moment, but if someone else comes along, she is exchangeable. I don't prefer Liz; I'm committed to her. We share a conviction that our relationship will never end and will improve each day. Without that, it will fail.

Governments display preference; they push policies which will attract votes rather than stand up against the tide of popular reasoning and state what is best for the economy, civil rights or justice. Society today needs leaders with conviction.

Passion Makes The Difference
The Bible has many stories of people who became great through conviction, going the extra mile, abandonment. Take, for example, the story of young David versus Goliath.

David was just a young kid when he took some tuna-on-rye-and-hold-the-mayo sandwiches down to his brothers, who were conscripts in the Israelite army fighting the hostile Philistines. The soldiers were still in camp when the giant Goliath appeared on a hilltop and challenged them to fight. The brothers' first reaction was to criticise David. Uncommitted people will always ridicule someone with commitment.

"What are you doing here, David? Have you just come to see the battle?"

If I were David I would have said, "What battle? You guys are too chicken to fight. I don't see a single arrow going anywhere. All you're doing is yelling insults at each other. What wimps!"

People who live by preference prefer to talk rather than take action.

What David did say was, "Who does this overgrown, ugly, OD'd on steroids think he is? Is there not a cause to fight for?" In other words, you have our homeland to protect - and, by the way, the king is willing to shower you with money, give his daughter to you in marriage and make you exempt from paying taxes ever again if you face that smelly brute.

David was motivated by a cause. He had passion. He walked up to that nine foot heathen with the attitude "This guy is too big to miss" and killed him. Passion and conviction, combined with risk-taking and abandonment, will bring you great rewards in every area of life. I've heard a lot of motivational speakers over the years, and the difference between a good speaker and a great speaker is their passion. You can see it, feel it. You can't explain it but you know when it's there. That's also what gives them their credibility.

I remember one day meeting a particular motivator who is a master at speaking on marketing strategies, sales and managerial skills. He was on the mobile phone putting out fires left, right and centre in his organisation.

When he got off the phone I asked, "Don't you have a team to do that stuff for you? Don't you teach this stuff?"

"It's easy to teach, Pat, it's a lot harder to do."

I thought to myself, "I'm never going to teach something that I can't do. When I'm doing it and I've got the heart to speak about it, people will know the conviction in my heart."

Contagious Abandonment
A positive side effect of adopting the spirit of abandonment is that it is highly contagious, and you can be responsible for launching other people towards their destinies.

Many sports champions, inspiring leaders and business pioneers have chased after their dreams and inspired others to follow them. Think of Rich deVos and Jay Van Andel. They started in Jay's basement as Ja-Ri and now have a worldwide network of over two million Amway distributors.

My life changed when I heard a frail old man speak to us at training college back in 1979. He poured his heart out. He had a desperate passion to improve the lives of teenagers.

Forget the generation gap; here was a man impacting the lives of people young enough to be his great-grandchildren.

He challenged us: "Who will take up the torch to love and heal the wounds of this broken generation? How many of you will take up the challenge to reach this discarded generation?"

That was the day I made my decision to work towards the betterment of the youth of our world. He was a man with a spirit of abandonment. I couldn't help but follow.

Perhaps your workplace is full of clock-watchers. They start at nine, stop for morning tea, lunch and afternoon tea, then go home at five. They simply turn up. They exist.

Then you walk in with a new spirit in your heart: abandonment. At first you will probably face ridicule.

"Why go the extra mile? It's not worth it."

"You're just crawling to the boss."

"Don't get carried away; it's just a job."

"Hey, slow down, you'll make us look bad."

Yet, in time, some of those colleagues will embrace your "now or never" attitude and pick up their pace. Forget the clock, we've got work to do.

I pray that you take on the spirit of abandonment. You'll never be the same again. When I think of the young people, the families and the business people on this planet who need help I burn with passion and conviction. Let me at 'em!

Let that be your desire too. Find your destiny and abandon yourself to it!

TAKE ACTION

1. Do you have a CAUSE to motivate you? Write it down.

2. When was the last time you did something for the first time?

3. What are your five most important convictions in life?
-
-
-
-
-

4. What risks can you take to launch yourself into your dream?

A QUICK LOOK AT BECOMING A RISK TAKER

1. Convictions give you purpose.

2. Possess the exhilarating spirit of abandonment - relinquish yourself to yield to an unrestrained impulse.

3. Success and life are risky.

4. Be a person of conviction rather than preference.

12.
KEEPING THE FIRE
IN YOUR BELLY

Motivation: that which incites to action, movement or motion.

The Collins Dictionary defines motivation as: "that which incites to action, movement or motion. To motivate, to incite." My definition is: "Having the fire inside you, the passion, the drive, the initiative and the excitement to do what needs to be done to make your life what you want it to be."

If your bank account has hit rock bottom and the bills keep piling up...the boss is asking you to put in a lot more work but on the same salary...the car just blew up and you can't afford to replace it...your teenager is skipping classes and hanging out with the wrong crowd...your parents won't stop fighting...the person you were engaged to just took off with someone else...what will help you stay motivated? There has to be some kind of reason to hang in there.

Motivation is a combination of a number of factors: your *mind* which decides what you want to achieve; your *will* which gives you the resolve to fulfil it; your *emotions* which will stir you to act; your *effort*, which is the amount of drive you're willing to put behind your goal; and your *action* , which is a culmination of the above.

> *Motivation is a huge factor in the betterment of ourselves.*

Motivation Climbs Mountains

Recently I was thinking laterally (another way of saying I was daydreaming) and I recalled the dream birthed in me when I started Youth Alive. It was a mammoth vision to put on a national music festival at a theme park for teenagers with lots of fun and activity.

I was inspired to turn my dream into reality when I attended a meeting where the speaker impacted me with a rousing message about faith. I hurriedly wrote down what I could see in my mind's eye. A huge music festival. Thousands of kids. Laughter. Excitement. Music. Loud music! People having the best time of their lives and being challenged to seek their life purpose and destiny. I was fired up.

I calculated the emotional and practical cost. It was huge. I had no money to do it and I'd never been involved in anything on such a grand scale before. Would the young people want to come? Would the musicians accept my invitation to be part of something so new? Would the venue work out all right? What about possible rejection and criticism? How would my small team of four people cope with it? Looking at my dream on paper I could see it was a huge task. There was going to be a mountain of work and organisation. Mt Everest was a speed hump by comparison. No money, no prior experience, no venue booked, no performers - just an idea. But the one key factor that caused this dream to become reality was the motivation to get it done. I had spoken at music festivals in various countries before so I began to think of the steps required to bring them together. I turned my thoughts into notes, got the team together and laid out the plan. We had started.

The reality (after much hard work) was that we did stage the music festival. It was arguably one of the greatest events ever held in our country, with such a widespread national impact that to this day we still get a lot of calls from people asking us to do it again.

Staying Motivated In The Tough Times
Athletes need victory to keep them going. They go from one medal to the next. It keeps them motivated. They recognise that motivation must be continuous. They also recognise that being motivated achieves nothing unless there is something to aim at.

*Motivation is fuelled by cause, driven
by vision and implemented by action.*

How can you stay motivated in the tough times? Here are some practical guidelines which will help you:

1. Input.

This includes inspirational and challenging books, tapes, speakers and other motivated people.

2. Overcoming.

Every victory gives you the courage and confidence to aim for the next one. It motivates you to aim for bigger, tougher victories. Develop a sense of overcoming in your heart.

3. Confidence.

There is nothing more de-motivating than lack of confidence.

4. Find Your Niche.

Take time to discover what you are good at. Go on a treasure hunt for the hidden gems and talents inside you. Chances are you'll be pleasantly surprised.

5. A Desire for Growth and Expansion.

Don't desire to stay where you are today. Have a willingness and passion to grow and expand. Have a desire to stretch beyond your current limitations.

6. Dress Right.

If you dress like a slob you'll feel like a slob. Dress like a motivated, going-somewhere person and you will feel motivated. What type of day do you want to have? Dress for that kind of day. Dressing right helps to motivate you.

Lost And Found

In my first year of youth training I was asked to go on a trip to Fiji. During the morning I went out shopping with my senior lecturer who was probably the greatest teacher I had ever had. We were having fun bargaining with store owners and buying things when all of a sudden he turned to me and said, "Pat, I'm not speaking tonight. You are."

Was I excited! What I wasn't going to do wasn't worth talking about.

He continued, "Pat, you've been out all day, so have a rest; sleep for half an hour."

I said, "No way. I'm going to prepare my message and get ready for tonight."

He kept saying to me, "Take a break, have a rest," but I was about to change the world with this message. It had to be perfect.

What I said that night didn't amount to a pile of beans. In fact, if there had been a pile of beans there I would have dived into it. My message was bad. It was badder than bad. So much for all that preparation. I got myself totally tongue-tied and knotted up. At the end of the night the lecturer came over to me. "I told you to rest, Pat," he laughed.

My confidence was totally shattered. I never wanted to be seen in public again.

The next day the lecturer and I went out for some more bartering. I was having fun until he said, "You're speaking tonight."

"No, I'm not!"

"Yes you are."

Then I realised the crowd was probably going to be bigger than the night before. "I'm not speaking!"

"You are. I'm the boss, you do what I say. But this time, go and have a rest first."

I did.

That night I got up to speak and - you guessed it - it was good. It was better than good. It was great. Eleven out of ten. I had made it. My confidence had been restored and I was a success.

At times your confidence will take a knock. When that happens there's only one thing to do: Get back up and keep doing what you intended to do anyway.

Leave Bashfulness Behind
Motivation and confidence have a lot to do with our

image of ourselves. If you have a low self-confidence you're going to be trapped in a life of frustration, unhappiness, stress and guilt.

But it is possible to rid yourself of those tormenting attitudes and to gain a healthy confidence. On that subject, take a look at Norman Vincent Peale.

As a young boy, Peale was skinny and painfully shy. He wanted to be tough and solid, but no matter how many milkshakes and banana splits he indulged in, he couldn't gain a pound. To make matters worse, he was a preacher's kid. That was an inhibiting factor for someone growing up in a country town in Ohio.

Every member of the Peale family was a performer in public, but a platform speaker was the last thing this kid wanted to be. "I was shy and bashful,"

Motivation is a continual process. It's not something that you do once.

he wrote later. "This self image of inadequacy might have gone on indefinitely had it not been for something that the professor said to me during my sophomore year in college. One day after I had made a miserable showing he told me to wait after class. Then he said, 'How long are you going to be bashful like this, a scared rabbit afraid of the sound of your own voice? You had better change the way you think about yourself, Peale, before it's too late!' "

You might think this was pretty heavy for a kid, but

this shy and bashful boy went on to become one of America's most popular preachers and writers.

Never Ending
Motivation is a continual process. It is not something that you do once. One inspirational business seminar or personal development book is not enough.

Think about it. You need healthy food and vitamins to stay healthy. You need sleep to stay fresh. You need petrol to run your car. You need input to keep your motivation up.

Motivation must be constantly invested in your life.

With constant motivation connected to a vision, goals and a positive attitude, the sky's the limit!

TAKE ACTION

1.Find some motivational tapes and listen to them on a regular basis to motivate you.

2. Keep your car glove compartment full of these tapes.

3. Find motivational books to read to keep yourself motivated. Even if you only read a page a day...READ.

A QUICK LOOK AT MOTIVATION

1. Motivation involves your mind, will, emotions, effort and action.

2. Motivation is a huge factor in reaching your destiny.

3. Motivation requires daily input: books, tapes, seminars, association with leaders, building dreams, self-talk, positive affirmations.

4. If you lose confidence, get back on your feet and keep doing what you intended to do anyway.

5. Find out what you are good at.

PART THREE:
THE OBSTACLES, CHALLENGES AND HINDRANCES

Every crisis is an opportunity...in disguise.

13.
WHEN YOU'RE GOING
THROUGH HELL...DON'T STOP!

*"Circumstances do not
make you what you are, they
reveal what you are."*
John Maxwell

A thousand conflicting thoughts and emotions ricocheted around inside my head and tugged at my heart. I looked up at the man who sat beside my hospital bed in silence reading a newspaper, his sarcastic smile saying, "I've got one over you, Mesiti!" He hadn't said a word all day. It was another one of his ploys to degrade and humiliate me.

What was going on? Here I was at the tender age of twenty-four, in my first youth leadership role since graduating from training college, a total emotional mess. The victim of verbal abuse, ridicule and unjust accusations; of being told day after day that I was an embarrassment, a hopeless speaker, a nobody who would never amount to anything. And there was my leader, a dictatorial, mean-spirited, cynical and hurtful man, enjoying every minute of it.

I thought of my young wife, Elizabeth, at home in our ramshackle, falling-apart house with our first newborn, Rebecca. I knew Liz was worried about what would happen to me - not knowing what lay ahead or whether I still had a career or not. I had already endured a childhood with alcoholic parents, going through constant shame and insecurity, but this was worse. This was hell on earth.

I had firmly believed my lifetime destiny was to make an impact on young people, but nothing had prepared me for this. Was it the end? Would I have to quit? Go and find an office job? Give up my passion to change lives?

Everything in me wanted to reach out and scream. I wanted to call my family and order some customised concrete shoes (I'm Italian, you know)! Anger wanted to rise up, reason tried to squash it down, confusion ran round and round. My brain felt like it was in a blender.

In the middle of this pain and uncertainty I made a very important decision. Today, with the luxury of more than ten years hindsight, I can clearly say that one thought changed my life. It made me the man I am today, relating to hundreds of thousands of teenagers and businesspeople each year.

What was the decision? I remember saying to myself: "I will refuse to get bitter. No-one will have the privilege of dictating to me how I will respond. I am going to keep sweet."

Bruce Springsteen had a song that went "Like a river

that doesn't know where it's going I took a wrong turn and just kept going". That's a tragedy. Life shouldn't be like that.

I eventually made it through that horrific episode and my youth work progressed. Was it easy? No. Did it take time to heal? Yes. But the important thing is I made it. I moved on to build the Youth Alive movement and speak into the lives of people all over the world. And I believe I'm a better person for it.

This pre-Promised Land experience, as I have since called it (because it felt like I was all alone in the wilderness), taught me a very valuable lesson. When it feels like you're going through "hell on earth" - a totally horrific experience - don't hang around. Don't even slow down. Keep on moving out of there as fast as you can. Look for the exit and run!

My destiny was far too important to surrender. My desire to help people meant everything to me. I had no Plan B to fall back on. It was this or nothing. So I put up with the ridicule and torment, got myself out of hospital, and concentrated on building an effective youth movement.

And what happened to the other guy? He hasn't been heard of since.

As Common As Air
Challenges - crises - are part of life. They are common to all of us. We can't live with them and we

can't live without them. I remember reading a book that said we're either in a crisis or heading towards one. Doesn't that make you feel good!

"The things which hurt instruct."
Benjamin Franklin

Crises come in different shapes and sizes. There are small, medium, large and extra-large challenges in life. They have different intensities and different timings - usually they arrive when they're least expected - and are seldom appreciated when they appear.

Crises often inflict stress and strain, but how we react to them determines how we will be once they're gone. With each test of our strengths and weaknesses, our abilities and personality, comes an opportunity for advancement. In the sporting world, for example, which athletes are selected to represent their nation? Those who have faced and conquered the most challenges.

One of the most unnatural responses in a time of "going through hell" is to welcome it. But it is not masochistic to believe that, as every crisis hits you, you are about to move ahead. It's all attitude. There's an interesting statement in the Bible: "Consider it pure joy when you face trials of many kinds, knowing that the testing of your faith develops perseverance, that perseverance once achieved brings you to maturity, complete and not lacking in anything" (James 1:2-4). That's a unique concept: when trials come it's development time. Character time. Perseverence time. So maintain your joy.

Crises Don't Kill Greatness

"The crisis of yesterday is the joke of tomorrow." **H. G. Wells**

The greatest baseball player of all time was Babe Ruth. A legend half a century ago, his record for the most home runs still stands today.

He was a man who experienced the highs of international fame - and the lows.

During one of his last major league games, the Braves against the Cincinatti Reds in Cincinatti, Babe was having a horror time. Not being as agile as he was in the early days, he fumbled throws and dropped catches. In one innings alone his mistakes gave away five runs to the Reds.

The crowd was getting hostile. Used to seeing him blitz the opposition, they were hissing, booing and yelling obscenities.

I can imagine Babe would have preferred to be anywhere but on that field.

As the Braves walked towards the dugout to commence another inning, a little boy jumped over the railing and raced across the grass, tears streaming down his face. He threw his arms around the legs of his hero.

Without stopping, the giant baseballer reached down, picked up the boy, hugged him, set him down and patted him gently on the head.

The noise from the grandstands came to an abrupt halt. The snickering stopped.

Babe continued his walk to the dugout and the boy ran back to his parents.

You could sense what the fans were thinking. In spite of having such a dismal day, Babe Ruth could still care about the feelings of a young boy.

Both had melted the hearts of the noisy crowd.

If an Olympic runner was right off the pace after the first lap of their race, they wouldn't walk off the track and go home.

The athlete pushes on to the finish line, always hopeful of winning a medal.

Bad days come to everyone. Dreamers move past them and keep going.

Don't Stop!
There is a tendency for people to want to "abandon ship" or "jump off the train while it's still in the tunnel". But my advice is: DON'T STOP! Keep on moving forward. Keep on progressing.

> *"Obstacles are those frightful things you see when you take your eyes off your goal."*
> *Henry Ford*

When the worst news you've ever had hits you - don't stop. When friends leave you because of a choice you've made - don't stop.

When you've shown your business to someone and they claim it will never work and slam the door in your face - don't stop.

When your kids come back from school with fifteen earrings in one ear, a ring in their nose and a chain joining them all together - don't stop.

When your teenager gets straight D's in their report card - don't stop.

When you've given as much as could be expected and you've been challenged to give more of yourself, your time and your finances - don't stop.

When your sure-fire plan just "sure-fired" on you - don't stop.

When you are feeling depressed, lonely and rejected and the hair dryer won't work...

When the business that you just invested all of your life savings in has closed down, the dog has fleas, the fridge is empty and the cat has worms...

And, ladies, when your husband neglects to take out the garbage, leaves his dirty clothes all over the floor, forgets your anniversary, leaves you to mind the kids while he goes out for a round of golf, and you've broken your nail - don't stop.

The temptation to give up is normal. Quitting requires a lot less effort than overcoming. But who wants to be "normal"?

Achievers, successful people, winners live beyond normal.

Don't settle for where you are; believe you can achieve more. Develop a "Never Give Up" attitude. Get angry at mediocrity. Pursue your life destiny with an unstoppable desire, so that when the next crisis explodes in your face you will keep on going, and going, and going.

"When I was young I observed that nine out of ten things I did were failures, so I did ten times more work."
George Bernard Shaw

TAKE ACTION

1. List the difficulties currently facing you.

2. How have you reacted at this point:

- despairingly?

- quit and given up?

- tried to ignore them?

- looked for a solution?

- determined to overcome?

3. Have you made any progress in solving them?

4. List three things you can do to overcome your difficulties.

A QUICK LOOK AT NEVER GIVING UP

1. Crises are common to all of us. Learn from them and use them as a springboard to your future.

2.Decide that you are in charge of your feelings and how you respond to circumstances.

3.Keep sweet.

4. When it feels like you're "going through hell", DON'T STOP.

14.
DON'T HANG AROUND
WITH PRAIRIE CHICKENS

*"You don't drown by falling
in the water, you drown
by staying there."*
Dr Edwin Louis Cole

"Nobody's perfect!"

This would have to be one of the most used phrases in the world today. And it's true. Nobody is perfect.

Many people rely on those three words as a cop-out because they're not willing to go after a higher level.

Some years ago I first read a brilliant book by Ted W. Engstrom called *The Pursuit of Excellence*. I liked it so much I have read it over and over again. It made

> *"The past should be a springboard, not a hammock."*
> **Edmund Burke**

me realise that we carry within us far more potential than we're willing to give ourselves credit for. Every time I flick through those dog-eared pages I am challenged to pursue excellence.

One of Engstrom's illustrations graphically demonstrates our lack of drive and courage. It is a story about a young American Indian brave who found an eagle egg and put it in a nest of prairie chickens.

The bird hatched and joined the brood of chickens. It was obviously different, with its majestic colours and big strong wings, but it grew up believing it was just another chicken. It scratched the dirt, pecked at seeds, clucked, cackled and thrashed its wings around to fly a few feet off the ground to a new pecking spot. Because that's what the chickens did.

One day it looked up into the heavens and saw a magnificent bird soaring with incredible skill. "What a beautiful bird. What is it?" it asked.

"That's an eagle," replied one of the chickens, "the chief of all the birds. But don't give it a second thought, you could never be like him."

And the eagle eventually died thinking he was a prairie chicken.

"Believe you are defeated, believe it long enough and it is likely to become a fact."
Norman Vincent Peale

It's the same with a lot of people today. The constant put-downs, the under-achievement mentality, the Tall Poppy Syndrome and the desire to keep ourselves at the same level as everyone else all prevent us from breaking out of our current situation.

If you've been going through a series of challenges it could be because there is little incentive in your world to rise above it. People aren't encouraging you to kick the dust off your feet and fly out of that dirty chicken coop up into the clear blue skies of opportunity. Well, I am!

An Eagle Inside
To break through the monotonous scratching around of life we need to realise that there is an eagle inside all of us. Every person has the power to exceed their limitations. A life of excellence is waiting for you.

What's holding you back? The fear of failing? That's the most common reason. Perhaps you've tried to conquer your problems before and nothing happened, so you're not confident of going through the struggles and hardship to try again.

But understand one thing: it's okay to fail.

Failing shows that you had the guts to try. Sitting back and wishing for a solution will get you nowhere. As one motivational book puts it, we fail our way to success.

"Failure is only the opportunity to begin again more intelligently."
Henry Ford

Every mistake and every event is a learning experience. John Wooden puts it like this: "It's what you learn after you know it all that counts, but you will never get to know it all if you never have a go. You never learn unless you pursue a more excellent life."

Blameititis

The Japanese have a principle: "Don't point the finger, find the solution." That could be why they are such a giant in manufacturing, technology and finance in the world today.

What they mean is this: don't go looking for people to tear strips off because another problem blew up in your face; instead, spend your energy looking for the answer.

It's natural to go on a witch hunt. Find the culprit and stone them! Chase them out of town! But if something has already happened it can't be undone.

Blame-chasing is wasted time and wasted energy. It keeps you focused on the problem and the past, not on the solution and the future. What often occurs is that other failings or mistakes from the past come flooding back into your mind at the same time. Instead of having to just deal with a month of poor sales or more bills than bucks, you are instantly reminded of all of the other times you missed the mark. And you feel even worse. A solution seems even further away.

Blameititis is a vicious cycle. Once you start thinking "someone's going to pay for this", you quickly move on to "I won't rest until I get them" and "I'll never trust anyone again". This in turn leads to "the whole world's against me" and "I might as well give up now, there's no way out". And that goes back to "someone's going to pay..."

To escape blameititis you have to burst out of the bubble. Accept the challenge, then logically work out how it happened and what

> *"Make a way, find a way or get out of the way."*
> Ted Turner

resources you have to work through or around it. Do you need more people or special skills? How will you get them? Can you keep operating while solving this crisis or does it have to be dealt with straightaway?

I'd Like To But...
If you don't properly cure blameititis it will spread like a sickly cancer into excuseitis. This is worse. It will give you 1001 reasons why you can't find an answer, can't keep progressing, can't achieve your goal, can't turn your dreams into reality.

"I'd like to but..."

Tragically, a huge number of people from all walks of life don't stand up against blameititis and excuseitis, and these develop into a far more crippling disease: paralysis. They give up. Everything is too hard. Life is just a blur of meaningless days and weeks doing the same meaningless things. They are, as I call them, the Walking Dead.

> *People who say it can't be done shouldn't interrupt those who are doing it.*

No matter how bad you feel, no matter how immense the problems are, no matter how long you've been wandering around looking for the exit — don't let yourself sink into nothingness and obscurity. Be accountable. When problems strike (they never tap you politely on the shoulder!) look for the solution ASAP, and, regardless of who caused it, you be the one who takes responsibility.

Attitude Controls Altitude

The two dejected lab assistants approached the inventor Thomas Edison. "Sir, we have just completed our 700th experiment and we still don't have an answer. We have failed."

"No, my friends, you haven't failed," Edison replied. "We now know more about this subject than anyone else alive and we are closer to finding the answer because we know 700 things not to do."

No-one is immune from mistakes. There isn't a

person alive who hasn't made a small or critical mistake. The key is to respond positively; to have the right attitude. Every day you need to be telling yourself, "I will not live a life of quiet desperation, fearful of challenges and change, and settling for mediocrity. I will live a life of excellence. I will have a go!"

Have a go. Give life your best shot. Realise that mistakes or failings are an education for you. That's the winning perspective you need to take.

Your environment, boss, job, family, peers, salary or current circumstances will not automatically deliver you a life of excellence. Your attitude will. People will knock you down, try to steal your dream, attempt to persuade you to stay where you are. But you will be protected by your attitude.

> *"What lies behind us and what lies before us are tiny matters compared to what lies within us."*
> *Ralph Waldo Emerson*

From The Inside Out
You might be thinking, "Pat, I've had too many bricks thrown at me in life." Well, the first thing to do is to pick up those bricks and build something with them. It's attitude.

Or you might be thinking, "I've heard all this before.

I don't need more motivating. I'm motivated already." I recall the day I asked a friend if he was going to attend a special seminar. "No," he replied, "that guy can't teach me anything, I've heard all of his lectures before." I thought the first thing my friend had done was ignore the attitude principles this speaker teaches, so he hadn't learnt at all. It comes back to attitude.

What is your attitude to what you have now? To your home? Do you think it's just an average place? Would you like to move on? If you don't keep it tidy and clean, mow the lawns and weed the gardens you might not ever go into a bigger more modern place. It's the same with a car, boat, caravan or off-roader.

Our lives are formed from the inside out. What is inside will come out. Attitudes are eventually expressed through our actions. Have you ever been motivated by a grump — I mean a full-on grump who puts people down, complains about life, frowns and expects the worst? It doesn't happen.

> *"He who stops being better stops being good."*
> *Oliver Cromwell*

What is your attitude to people? If they are just numbers and you don't care much for them, people won't be drawn to you. Your attitude determines how people will respond.

The famous American business tycoon Andrew

Carnegie paid a million dollars to Charles Schwab because of his incredible it-can-be-done attitude and ability to motivate people. In Schwab's words, "A man can succeed at almost anything for which he has unlimited enthusiasm."

The principles for developing a successful life are quite simple. Many of those I have taken hold of are easy enough to be taught to children, and yet adults struggle to interpret them. Take the following steps, for example, and think about how they would change your current way of thinking:

1. GATHER new and correct information to empower and inform you.

2. DISCARD incorrect or negative preconceptions and thought patterns.

3. TELL others the truth; don't prejudge people or lie to them.

4. REPEAT positive messages to yourself.

5. RENEW your mind with good input.

6. ASSOCIATE with people with a right mindset and attitudes.

7. ADMIT your past mistakes and wrong mindsets.

8. ACCEPT right mindsets.

Grab hold of these principles and you'll be able to launch into the air and start soaring like an eagle!

TAKE ACTION

1. Make it an aim to discard negatives and renew your mind.

2. Actively implement this action.

3. Are there relationships hindering you from reaching your destiny? Make sure you cut them off.

A QUICK LOOK AT FLYING LIKE AN EAGLE

1. Believe that you were created for greatness.

2. Blame-chasing is wasted energy and time.

3. Blameititis is a vicious cycle that gets you nowhere. Get rid of it before it spreads.

4. Our lives are formed from the inside out. Right attitudes lead to right actions.

5. There's an eagle in you. Learn to fly!

15.
MISSING THE MARK

Failure is success turned inside out.

J oe Sorrentino started life on the violent streets of Brooklyn in downtown New York City. He was a high school dropout, fought in gangs and was dishonourably discharged from the Marine Corps. All this he achieved by the age of 20. He was the original BA - Bad Attitude.

Out of the army, Joe went back to the streets. He hung out with his gang, the Condors. Then one night he was in a vicious fight and had a shocking experience. "We were out in a rumble and I saw my hero's head blown off. I had to identify the body for the police and I suddenly realised something had changed my life."

That day Joe saw that despite their bravado he and his friends were not supermen, but vulnerable human beings - real people who live and die. And he knew it wouldn't be long before he too ended up in a body bag. Joe decided to take a huge step. He recalled the words of one of his teachers who said he could be a good student if he really wanted to (if you're an educator, take note of the lifetime effect a teacher's words had on the life of a young, impressionable boy). So Joe Sorrentino, tough, street-smart gang leader, went back to school. Can you imagine the mocking he must have received from his ever-so-tough friends? But the motivation was there. Joe enrolled in night school to catch up on the three years of schooling he had missed, and during the day he earned his keep by plucking chickens. The gang leader even had an honest job!

Joe received his high school diploma and decided to get as far away as possible from his environment. California is about as far as you can get from New York, so off he went to UCLA. The first year was tough, but he struggled on and got a scholarship. By his junior year he was doing well. In his senior year he was elected Student Body President!

Rather than indulge himself with the rewards of his hard work and accept a good position with one of the various companies that approached him, Joe went back into the Marines. "I wanted to go back and right a wrong. I left a bad mark and wanted to change it to a better one. So I put in a year of active service and two years of inactive. I got an honourable discharge."

Keep failure in perspective.
It's a learning process, not an end in itself.

The former gang leader's next giant step was to go to Harvard Law School. This required another adjustment; his speech and mannerisms caused people to think he was part of the Harvard maintenance crew rather than a law student. "I kept working on my vocabulary and after three years I won the School's forensic competition."

Joe was selected as Class Valedictorian and that role included giving the commencement speech at Harvard. *Time* magazine reprinted the speech, which included these thoughts:

"There are certain qualities in human beings that cannot be measured by aptitude tests, such as courage, drive, determination and creativity. No matter what you are told negatively on a scale of measurement, you should not become discouraged. Low estimates can't dim the flame of high inspiration. A test result can be a very unromantic decree. You can tell a person at a young age, `You can't be anything'. I knew that was not necessarily how it had to be. It could have been for me, but I had made up my mind not to let it. I had seen how life could have ended on the street or in the county morgue."

Joe Sorrentino, a dead-end kid from the rough and tough streets of New York, became a juvenile court judge in Los Angeles County.

Joe's is a remarkable story. But it can be repeated - by you.

Don't stay at Camp Failure. Don't allow past

> *"The greatest mistake you can make in life is to fear you'll continually make one."*
> *Albert Hubbard*

mistakes to hold you back. Keep moving. You'll get tired, you'll have mud on your shoes and at times you'll want to stop. But just around the next bend could be Success City.

One Of The Best Words In The English Language

Rich DeVos and Jay Van Andel, co-founders of the amazing Amway empire, have a very insightful view of failure. Van Andel calls it a marvellous word. DeVos says it is one of the best words in the English language. Why? Jay explains:

"Failure is the bridge. Sure, some people stop in the middle of it and jump off, but others recognise that the bridge has a brand new plot of land at the other end. Just keep on walking. Don't be afraid if you find yourself on another bridge some day, and another, and another. They all lead somewhere.

"The idea is not to stop walking and, most importantly, to know where it is that you want to go."

I'm sure these two billionaires know exactly what they are talking about. They have crossed many bridges and mountains to build a huge business empire.

Keep failure in perspective; don't let it ruin your motivation or your life. Carl Lewis has lost some races in his time and Michael Jordan has missed some baskets. Baseball legend Babe Ruth hit the all-time record of 740 home runs in his career, yet he also set the record for being struck out the most times. Corporate presidents have made wrong decisions. Every public speaker has had a bad day. (Trust me on that one - they have!)

Read about the life of Abraham Lincoln and you'll find a man who was hit - pulverised would be a more appropriate word - by failure for most of his life: bankruptcy, business

> *"If at first you don't succeed you're running about average."*
> **M. H. Alderson**

collapse, poverty, the tragic death of his young wife and countless election losses. But he, like Lewis, Jordan and Ruth, never gave up.

Learn From Failure

Don't base your confidence and motivation on failure. One bad day won't affect your whole life. When the attendance at one of our recent youth rallies was noticeably low, I felt so depressed that I wanted to quit. One of my friends came over and said encouragingly, "One bad day, one bad crowd doesn't mean the end of a major movement. Let's learn from it." He was right, and that's exactly what we did.

Here are six principles for beating failure rather than letting it beat you:

1. Learn from failure.

Have you heard the adage "Love 'em and leave 'em"? Well, I have my own saying about failures: "Learn from 'em and leave 'em". Learn from what took place, then leave. Don't let your mind dwell on it. Leave it in the basket marked Learnt.

2. Don't set up camp in your mistakes.

A lot of people make a mistake, get bogged down and then pitch their tent there. They continue living on the campsite of failure.

My advice is simple: GET OUT OF THERE! Keep moving on to a new plot of land and build an empire there, something other than a tent which can get blown away by the winds of competition, compromise or challenge.

3. Don't rehash past losses.

One of the saddest things to me is people rehashing past losses and hurts. It's like living in a rubbish dump. They keep stirring that pile of rotting trash around and around, and it stinks. If I rehashed the negatives every time I had a bad day speaking to people I'd never get up to speak again!

Don't regurgitate past failures. Bury them and throw away the shovel. Don't come back and dig them up again.

4. Keep working on it.

Maybe you've just failed to reach a sales or budget target, you've lost a major client or you've been out night after night trying to discuss your business with people who don't want to work with you. Perhaps it's something smaller, like putting on weight when you're trying to shake it off, or not completing a report on time. Even if you don't succeed, keep working on it.

5. View failure from new angles.

Ask yourself: "Was it failure or lack of preparation? Was it the wrong timing? Did I consider all the options?" It might not have been failure; it might have been a miscalculation. It might even be an opportunity to see your obstacles from a different viewpoint and achieve a greater success than you originally expected.

6. Remember: failure is not final.

If at first you don't succeed, join the line. Tomorrow is a new day. Try, try and try again.

The following words of Teddy Roosevelt relate to confidence and failure and they're just as powerful today as they were when this great man first uttered them:

"It's not the cynic who counts, not the man who points out how the strong man stumbled or where the doer of deeds could have done better. The credit belongs to the man who is actually in the arena, whose face is marred by dust and sweat and blood, who strives valiantly...who knows the great enthusiasms, the great devotions, and spends himself in a worthy cause, who at the best knows in the end the triumph of high achievement and who, at the worst, if he fails, at least fails on daring greatly, so that his place shall never be with those cold and timid souls who know neither victory or defeat."

That is a powerful and awesomely true statement.

More Motivation Killers
Failing to beat failure is a massive hindrance to motivation. Passively lying down and accepting second best as your lot in life, rather than taking the knocks and scrapes and moving on, drags you down into defeat. Dig your heels in and resist!

Another hindrance is the only kind of party you don't want to get invited to: a pity party. Wallowing in self-pity over a failed goal or missed target is a sure motivation killer. It will sap you of energy and confidence overnight, with worse consequences than a hangover.

Sometimes you can allow yourself to believe what others say about you and to convince you you're a liar. In the Disney movie *The Lion King*, which is a powerful story of destiny, little Simba believes that he is the cause of the death of his beloved father. The real murderer is his wicked uncle, who wants to steal the throne, but little Simba believes the lie spun by his evil relative and gives away his right to the kingship. For years he lives under the bondage of that untruth until one day he realises that he really is the Lion King and that a great and powerful destiny belongs to him. He returns to take back what is rightfully his.

Believing the lies or rumours spread by other people, especially those who are envious of your conviction to pursue a better life, can take away your motivation. Be careful.

The people who are most vulnerable to failure are those who lack a healthy sense of identity. It is imperative that you understand who you are, what you are, why you are meant to be, where you are going. You are a unique person, a one of a kind, with a special worth and the ability to make a huge impact on the lives of those around you. Believe it. It's true.

What can you motivate yourself to do today that you haven't done before? What is the cause that propels you forward? What is your target? Your life ambition? What steps are you taking to reach that dream? What books are you reading? What tapes are you listening to? What people are you hanging around? Whose voices are you listening to?

When you know who you are and where you're going you won't lose time and energy seeking constant reaffirmation from others. You'll be able to look failure in the face, regroup and move on after your dream.

Regardless of your past, you have a dynamic future waiting for you - AND YOU DESERVE IT!

TAKE ACTION

1. Have you ever felt like a failure? (It's not necessary to make a list. If you're like me you could write your own book on that subject.)

2. What did you learn from past mistakes?

3. Did that knowledge help you to face new challenges?

4. What new attitudes have you discovered towards failure as a result of reading this chapter?

5. How will you handle failure in the future?

A QUICK LOOK AT FAILURE

1. Failure is NOT final.

2. One failure doesn't mean you have to quit everything. One bad day won't affect your whole life.

3. Don't bog down in your mistakes and pitch your tent there.

4. You only have to succeed one more time than all the times you've failed in order to make progress.

16.
SAYING HELLO
AND GOODBYE

"Carpe diem! Carpe diem!"
("Seize the day! Seize the day!")
From the movie
Dead Poets Society.

A crisis is a temporary chapter in your life, and you can shorten its time frame by choosing to tackle it head-on. When "normality" is suddenly replaced by "extreme difficulty", you need to summon every atom of boldness and face the storm.

You are going to have to be tough and courageous and display a far greater tenacity and determination than before.

Don't allow this saga to distract you from your future. Don't let it make you bitter rather than better.

Say to yourself: "I will stand! I will endure this challenge and learn from it. It will promote me to even greater heights."

Such a decision, a decision of empowerment, grips the emotions and builds mental strength.

The opposite response, capitulating and beating a hasty retreat, causes the soul and mind to degenerate into the miry black waters of misery, self-pity and failure.

From this decisive position of strength comes the need to understand how to confront your challenges, and the person I regard as an expert in that field is a man of great faith and integrity, Dr Edwin Louis Cole.

Dr Cole is the founder and president of the Christian Men's Network, based in Texas.

Entering And Leaving
Dr Cole is an authority on the subject of crisis and I thoroughly recommend his books. One of them, *Entering and Leaving Crisis*, details an incredible principle which has the power to accelerate our growth. It has to do with how we leave experiences behind and enter new ones.

Dr Cole explains that how we leave childhood determines how we enter adolescence.

How we leave school determines how we enter the work force.

How we leave one relationship determines how we enter the next.

How we leave a job determines how we enter another.

How we leave singleness determines how we enter marriage.

Every time I think of my trip through "hell" over ten years ago I'm reminded of this principle.

Without knowing it, I said goodbye to negativity and hurt and was able to enter the next phase of my career with a right spirit.

How we leave a crisis will determine how well we cope with the next one. This is why kids who suffer abuse as children leave childhood and enter adolescence with the same feelings.

To move in we first need to move out.

They leave home then inflict the same pains on their own kids in turn.

Leaving is important.

To leave a challenge behind means not taking the "excess baggage" with you - baggage such as negativity, criticism, loneliness and betrayal.

Failing to leave means dragging that unnecessary luggage through life.

This process can be distorted. Some people facing serious situations think that by ignoring or dropping them they will be automatically solved. Wrong. That's not leaving; that's running away.

You can't run away from you. Where you go, your problems go too. For example, an executive who is unjustly accused of wrongdoing and fired from his position may be filled with anger, self-pity, mistrust and a deep sense of injustice. But unless he leaves those negative, draining thoughts and emotions behind, he will take them into his next job, and this will seriously affect his performance.

> *It's the person who crosses the line who wins the medal.*

What challenges or crises are you facing right now? Do you want to leave them better rather than bitter? It is not wrong to feel hurt, but how you respond to that hurt makes all the difference. You have to see past the circumstances to where you are going - like a hurdler who knows he can only cross the finish line after he has jumped over the barriers.

Follow your dream, don't get stuck in your nightmares.

Time And Chance

Just as important as entering and leaving is the decision to "hang in there". Tenacity during crises can produce those serendipities of life when we find new opportunities in the midst of trials. Our time and chance to move to a higher level can occur right when we're wondering how we are going to make it through.

I pioneered Youth Alive with another youth worker who was my senior. Suddenly he resigned, and, although I was plunged into a personal crisis as a result, my time and chance had come. I seized the opportunity to reach my destiny.

In the movie *Dead Poets Society*, Robin Williams, playing an eccentric private boys school teacher, tells his students to grab opportunities: "Carpe diem! Carpe diem! Seize the day!" There is no better time than now.

William Arthur Ward said: "Real optimism is aware of problems but recognises solutions, knows about difficulties but believes they can be overcome, seizes the negatives but accentuates the positives, is exposed to the worst but expects the best, has reason to complain but chooses to smile."

Crisis Creates Quality

As I mentioned earlier, you need to realise that crises are normal. Don't freak out the next time the bottom falls out of your world.

For a start, stay productive. Keep your mind active. If the challenge will allow you to maintain your daily schedule, keep going. Focus on your ultimate goal. Realise that all things are temporary and will pass by.

Decide to leave each crisis with the same attitude you want to have when you enter the next phase of your life.

Keep sweet in the heat. When a piece of carbon goes through a series of processes involving immense heat and pressure it transforms into a diamond. Pressure, or crisis, has created a thing of beauty.

When first discovered, a diamond bears little resemblance to how it will look after being cut and polished. It goes from a dirty, dull chunk of rock to a sparkling prism of colour and light. Gold and silver ores are dug from the earth, but before they become things of value, they must be refined in intense heat to burn off the dross. So, too, we are refined by the heat and pressure of life.

I get opportunities to speak all over the world. Each time I see racism, violence and discrimination taking place. I get a close look at the hurt and suffering of people, from the ghettos right up to the stately homes. I meet the victims of sexual, emotional and mental abuse, the ones who have been let down, the dreamers who have had their dreams taken away, the people who have been savaged by criticism and ridicule, and those who have toiled tirelessly for ages without being rewarded.

Having experienced some of those injustices I know how they feel. And I know that these times refine you, like a precious metal being purified, so you become someone better. Ask yourself: Do I have a destiny? If the answer is yes (and it should be) then don't let anybody without one steal yours.

A group of marathon runners all leave the starting line at the same time, but not all of them will last the distance. It's the person who crosses the line who wins the medal. Spectators, fans and coaches can cheer and clap, but only the competitor tastes the joy of victory and the thrill of the moment.

We need to endure to the end to become more precious, more beautiful, more valuable to ourselves and our world. I hope that by understanding this you will have the courage to become better than your best.

Injustices will come. We live in an unfair world. But you are able to make the difference.

And remember: if it feels like you're between a rock and a hard place - don't stop! You're leaving lesser things behind and progressing to a greater level in life. Remember: it's how you enter that new level that determines success of future levels.

Decide to leave each crisis with the same attitude you want to have when you enter the next phase of your life.

TAKE ACTION

1. List the attitudes and feelings you'd like to have when you enter the next phase or circumstance in your life.

2. Decide that this is how you will leave your current challenge or growth phase.

3. If you are facing difficulties do your best to:

• Accept that crises are normal...and temporary

• Stay productive. Maintain your usual daily schedule if possible

• Keep your mind active

• Stay focused on your ultimate destination

A QUICK LOOK AT ENTERING AND LEAVING CRISIS

1. Crises are temporary.

2. How you leave one circumstance dictates how you will enter the next one.

3. Make a decision of empowerment: "I will stand! I will endure and learn from it. It will promote me to greater heights."

PART FOUR:
BECOMING THE
BETTER YOU

*"He that would govern others
first should be the master
of himself."
Phillip Massinger*

17.
WANTED: HEROES AND ROLE MODELS

"The credit belongs to the man who is actually in the arena."
Theodore Roosevelt

T he young high school student stood up in the crowd just as I was about to start talking. "You!" he called sharply. "I want to ask you a question."

"Yeah, sure," I replied, mimicking his cocky swagger.

The boy fired three questions at me relating to life values. His beliefs were way off course and I told him so. He thanked me and sat down.

"Get up!"

He was on his feet in microseconds.

"Why did you ask me those questions?"

I will never forget what he said. "I've been coming to this school for seven years and they keep telling me to make up my own mind. They say you'll work it out sooner or later. How can I make up my own mind when nobody will show me how to live?"

No-one at that school had the guts to stand up and say, "I will lead, you follow me".

The greatest human being and the greatest leader who ever lived was Jesus Christ. When he said "follow me" people walked away from their careers and changed the world. Think about it - in three years Jesus taught twelve close friends as much as he could; they then imparted the dream to hundreds more who went on to reach thousands. And now, 2,000 years later, Christianity is in every nation on earth. That's powerful networking!

You need to be able to say "follow me" to your spouse, your children, your business partner and employees, your football or baseball team. In being assertive, conquering crises and reaching out for dreams, you have direction. You are taking them somewhere.

> *The nations of the world are crying out for people to say "follow me".*

When people hear the two almost-endangered words "follow me" they are usually receptive and willing to respond. People long to follow a leader with a high purpose.

Leaders Worth Following
I've discovered that the kind of leaders I want to emulate all display the same characteristics. Here's how to be like them:

1. Have a positive outlook.

In my last book, *Wake Up And Dream*, I wrote about an old Chinese sage who met two travellers leaving a town.

The first man asked, "What is the town like that I am going to?" to which the sage replied, "What is the town like that you are coming from?" "Oh, it's evil, wicked and disgusting." "Well," said the sage, "where you're going is probably much the same".

A while later he met the second traveller who asked the same question. Again the sage responded, "What is the town like that you are coming from?" "Oh, it's beautiful, the people are wonderful and the weather is fine." "Well, the town you seek is much like that."

Yet both men were on their way to the very same town!

Your outlook determines your output. And remember, leaders are followed. At all times keep a positive outlook.

2. When you're on the right track, stay there.

To put it another way, if all the lights are green, keep going until you get a red light. As the Bible says, "a double-minded man is unstable in all his ways". One of the killers of leadership is indecisiveness and unnecessary shifts in philosophy and direction. Stay on the right track.

3. Set a standard of excellence.

Everything can improve. Set high standards and people will reach them. Set low standards and people will stoop to them. People aspire to and follow the standards we set.

Years ago at Youth Alive we were more relaxed about the posters, newsletters and signs we produced for our concerts. One day we noticed spelling mistakes and other typos creeping in. I set a much higher standard, which everyone on the team rose to. Tighter proofreading and triple-checking of artwork not only produced a better product, but saved us money and time in reprint costs.

4. Ignore the critics.

I dislike the term "constructive criticism". It's often an excuse for pessimists and cynics to rubbish your desire to improve. In my field there are many so-called experts who sit back and analyse everything I'm doing, then want to butt in. Sports commentators and spectators make great critics, but put them in the arena and see how well they perform!

5. Be results-oriented.

Great leaders love results. Employees and fellow

workers love results. Make sure that as a leader you are able to monitor and gauge your results. Expect results, breakthroughs, increase, more profit. Don't be busy just for the sake of being busy. Make sure there is product out of your labours, not just activity.

6. Encourage, encourage, encourage.

I love my team; they're loyal, hard workers who have their own visions as well as being part of mine. I like to pat them on the back and offer words of thanks when they least expect it. It fires them up for days.

Encouragement means overlooking people's weaknesses and highlighting their strengths. For example, I can guarantee that if you tell your spouse to lose weight or look like someone else, they will feel very depressed and achieve nothing. Tell them how great they are and that they have the get-up-and-go to attempt anything and they probably will.

7. Help people to grow.

Before I started my career working with young people I had odd jobs in a factory and shovelling concrete. Looking at me, all five foot nothing of me, you might think, "How did Mesiti manage to hold down jobs which required so much physical labour?" I had two good bosses who taught me everything I needed to know.

8. Be disciplined.

Discipline is one of those words we love to hate. But to aspire to greatness we need to discipline our time, activity and, most importantly, ourselves. Discipline is not your enemy. Make it your friend.

On my plane travelling I have sometimes gazed out the window at the clouds. How many boring clouds do you need to see! Read, study, meditate, make use of your time. Discipline is like a rudder to a ship, it helps you steer to your destination. And as I heard someone say "He who will not answer to the rudder will answer to the rocks."

9. Have a joyful, happy nature through the good and the bad.

Nothing is worse than a "wet blanket" leader. A joyful disposition doesn't mean you are a clown or court jester, it is a character thing. It is contagious, motivating and uplifting. It affects the way you talk to people, deal with them, and motivate them.

10. Aspire to something greater than yourself.

All great leaders have had a cause.

11. Be My Coach

There is one other quality of strong leadership that is absolutely vital. A true leader knows how to be led.

There is a pastor in Sydney, Australia, who has built a church from forty people in a small school hall to thousands attending sixteen services each Sunday and fills the biggest auditorium in the area. Brian Houston is a visionary and one of my great friends. Actually, he's my best friend.

His church is impacting the nation of Australia and numerous other churches overseas. He has a vision to change the world. That's why Brian is a mentor to me. I want to change the world too.

Every time we get together he challenges me. I tell him what I've been doing and he spurs me on to greater heights. More than that, he is a very wise man with a lot of commonsense. He shows me how I can get closer to my dreams. Brian is my head coach. He is a focused and strong leader with a passion and determination to release others into their full potential in life.

Everybody needs a coach. While the world needs strong leaders, strong leaders know they need mentors. Your coach can be straight, direct and open with his players and is always concerned for what is best for the team and individual. Brian is that kind of guy.

I remember an episode in my late teens when I turned up at the start of the football season feeling cocky. What I didn't know about football hadn't been thought of yet. Out stepped the new coach and all hell broke loose.

"Mesiti, fifty push-ups."

"Mesiti, fifty sit-ups."

"Mesiti, sprint around the field."

I staggered back, dripping with sweat, hurting all over. We didn't need to train; we were the best. What was this guy on about? More push-ups, more sprint training, more sit-ups, and on it went. I wanted to scream at him, throw his stupid whistle over the fence, gag his mouth.

"Now we'll work on the basics," he said.

The what? Hey, chum, we've been playing football since we could crawl; we don't need any of that. All night I punished my body with tackling practice, ball passing, kicking, and more sprinting and sit-ups. The coach was definitely on the Wanted list.

But before too long that coach turned a pack of headstrong individuals into a very good team. We trained three or four times a week right through the pre-season. One evening I asked him, "Why is it that we have to train so hard for a ninety minute game?" "To win" was his answer. And win we did.

One weekend we came up against the most feared team of all. I was petrified. "Coach, have you seen who they've got on their team?"

"No, I'm too busy looking at who I've got in mine. They might be great individuals, but you're a great team."

They still beat us, but towards the end of the season we met again. We were peaking, they had plateaued.

The thrill of victory was fantastic.

Great leaders don't just happen. They are moulded and developed by a coach.

Pat Riley is an all-time great coach. His LA Lakers basketball team virtually owned the NBA in the '80s until their reign was ended by the Detroit Pistons, who were subsequently unseated by the Chicago Bulls. Riley got people like Magic Johnson and made them great. He challenged his team to become one of the best in basketball history, and they did. Their greatness affected many others who were rising through the ranks.

In his book *The Winner Within*, Riley says: "You'll never rouse the winner within by making people feel they're a fill-in for sideline greatness." The best coaches bring out the best in you.

Call it purpose or destiny, call it what you want to, for Nelson Mandela it was the freedom of his nation. For me at Youth Alive it is seeing young people find their purpose in living. Whatever it is - aspire to it.

Find A Mentor

Find a coach you can follow - someone you can confide in, who will push you along, equip you, teach you. And remain teachable. Following a coach is one of the keys to becoming a coach for others.

People everywhere are looking for a mentor. One of the most amazing scenes I've ever witnessed was at a concert where the auditorium was filled with 7,000 screaming, crazy teenagers. These kids were tough. Everywhere I looked were broken teeth, black eyes, scarred faces and tattoos...and the guys looked even worse!

I was backstage with another man who has a huge influence on my life, Brian Houston's father Frank. Frank Houston has been in the ministry for about fifty years and he's still as fired up as an eighteen year old. Here he was, flouting any generation gap, stepping out in front of a maniac audience. He started speaking and soon had them laughing, crying, even doing both at once. Then he began to speak from the heart about life issues and the hall went quiet. He challenged them to change their ways.

Literally hundreds crammed up against the stage. Metalheads put away their aggression, girls who had been abused came forward weeping, outrageously-dressed mods moved up quietly with their heads hung low and skaters took off their hats in respect. All they wanted was a mentor, a coach, a person they could put their trust in. And they found that in a man old enough to be their grandfather!

Find a role model, a mentor, a person who is doing something better than you are. Spend time with those who stretch and challenge you. Let them prod you, push you, enthuse you, inspire you. Then you do the same for others.

In his brilliant book *Be All You Can Be*, John C. Maxwell adds more advice on how to become a key leader. "If we look up to a person who is reaching his or her potential, if we give

Give up the small or trivial things in your life to make way for new and far greater things.

up anything that hinders us from being our best, if we fire up our desires until we are no longer satisfied, and if we show up to our challenges and not become fearful, then we will go up," says Maxwell.

"We will go up to the top of our potential, but only after we look up, give up, fire up and show up."

And how true that is.

TAKE ACTION

1. Find a mentor.

2. Associate with that mentor.

3. Have the courage to receive correction and the strength to implement what your coach says. Remember, a coach won't always tell you what you want to hear, but what you need to hear.

A QUICK LOOK AT ROLE MODELS

1. You need to be able to say "follow me" to your spouse, children, business employees, sports team, etc.

2. Develop the qualities of a strong leader.

3. Great leaders don't just happen. They are moulded by a coach.

4. Find a mentor to inspire you to new heights.

18.
GOING WHERE NO
MAN HAS GONE BEFORE

A leader is a guide, conductor,
commander - the foremost
horse in the team.

In 1987 *Time* magazine asked in a cover story, "Who's In Charge?" It answered its own question by saying, "The nation calls for leadership and there is no-one home." What a tragic indictment of modern Western civilisation.

Consider this: as you decide to be accountable for your life and pursue your destiny, as you summon the courage and tenacity to face turmoil head-on, as you develop the qualities of a leader, you will become an incredible asset to your family, workplace, community, city and nation.

John W. Gardner, in *No Easy Victory*, states: "Leaders have a significant role in creating the state of mind that is society. They can serve as symbols of the moral unity of society. They can express the values that hold society together. Most importantly, they can achieve and articulate goals that lift people out of their petty preoccupations, carry them above the conflicts that tear society apart, and unite them in the pursuit of an objective worthy of their best efforts." What a powerful truth!

It's a simple fact of life that nations cannot live together without leaders. Your company needs leaders. Your sporting team needs a coach and captain. Wherever there is more than one person someone needs to lead. Otherwise chaos becomes the order of the day.

What Makes A Great Leader?
Someone once asked me, "How do I know if I'm a leader?" My reply was, "Turn around and see if anyone's following".

A much deeper question is this: "How can someone become a great leader?" This is often asked by those who look in awe at men and women who have achieved greatness, and by those who aspire to join their ranks. To answer it we need to look at what leadership is all about.

The role of a leader is changing in the '90s. The old system of the dictator beating up on timid, fearful and reluctant employees has gone.

The Collins Dictionary says a leader is "a guide, conductor, a commander. The foremost horse in the team". I like that. He's not the only horse, but he's the one at the front urging the others along, pulling them along, causing them to go faster and further than they have before.

A dictator threatens, abuses and uses force or fear to

motivate. A leader finds your potential and releases you into it through training and development and by challenging you to stretch further than you've ever gone before.

Today's great leaders are men and women who empower and train people, not members of an elite hierarchy that is distant, phoney and can't be related to.

A lot of my friends love Star Trek. I like the motto at the start of each show: To boldly go where no man has gone before. That's what a leader does - pioneering new ventures, starting new enterprises, creating new opportunities and empowering people to participate in them. Giving people a sense of destiny. Motivating them with a cause. Leading them to their full potential.

It is lack of leadership that causes companies and organisations to falter, to become average, even to disappear altogether. Leaders are the spark plugs that get the whole thing going. They provide the spontaneity, the burn, the momentum and impetus. Take a spark plug out of a car engine and all you have is scrap iron.

> *"A leader is a person who has the ability to get others to do what they don't want to do, and like it."*
> *Harry Trueman*

Leaders Make Things Happen

I don't think there can be just one definition of leadership because the qualities required for the task are many and varied. Some are captured in the powerful and penetrating insights of great leaders of the past.

The Emperor Napoleon, for example, said, "A leader is a dealer in hope." Mahatma Gandhi said, "To put up with misrepresentation and stick to one's guns, come what may, this is the essence of leadership." The great warrior-leader Hannibal typified this spirit as he pondered how to lead his army over the Alps to invade Rome: "I will find a way or I will make one."

These statements all describe vital components of leadership.

However, I have seen one very obvious common feature in the lives of great leaders, past and present, and that is an ability to make things happen. To help people be better than their best and become meaningful contributors to an organisation or society.

What sort of things does a leader make happen? John Adair, in his book *Effective Leadership*, identifies three: "The good leader is one who works as a senior partner with other members to achieve the task, build the team and meet individual needs." Good leadership:

1. Helps people achieve their goals.

2. Builds and maintains a healthy team spirit, vision and focus.

3. Helps individuals to reach their full potential in life.

The free flowing "mix" of these qualities creates growth and expansion, to the benefit of both the leader and the followers.

Decision, Decisions
One characteristic of the "new" kind of leader is the ability to be part of a decision-making process, not the only decision-maker. Sure, the leader sets the vision and the strategy, but in order to achieve that dream he needs to work as a team with others, harnessing strengths, building on weaknesses and understanding the true value and input of other people.

For this to be effectively achieved leaders must:

1. Trust in their own ability as well as trusting in team members to be able to make decisions and be forward-thinkers.

2. Communicate the vision powerfully, openly and clearly.

3. Hold others accountable and be accountable to

others.

4. Input into the lives of team members, which means leaders need to be fed so that they in turn can feed others.

5. Maintain loyalty and never play people off against each other or discredit them in public.

6. Get to know people as people, not just workers or colleagues. Building friendships is imperative to being a leader. One of the things we enjoy as a team at Youth Alive is that we're all good friends - a lot more than just work associates.

Much More Than Management

Leadership is not management. Leaders can often be good managers, but good managers are not necessarily good leaders.

While management involves analysis, calculation, method, timetables and systems, leadership is more motivation, personality, vision, entrepreneurial sense and spirit.

Author Ted Engstrom, who has written a book specifically about leadership, makes the following distinctions:

Leadership is a quality.
Management is a science and an art.

Leadership provides vision.
Management supplies realistic principles.

Leadership deals with concepts.
Management relates to functions.

Leadership exercises faith.
Management has more to do with fact.

Leadership seeks effectiveness.
Management strives for efficiency.

Leadership is an influence for good among potential resources.
Management is the co-ordination of available resources organised from maximum accomplishment.

Leadership provides direction.
Management is concerned about control.

Leadership thrives on finding opportunity.
Management succeeds on accomplishment.

Similarly, Peter Wagner writes: "Leadership catches concepts, vision and overall direction. Once those are established, management sees that it is done. Leadership decides where we are going and why. Management figures out how to get there."

Managers don't inspire, leaders do. General

Macarthur was not a manager. Martin Luther King was not a manager. Jesus Christ was not a manager.

Warren Bennis, in his outstanding book *On Becoming a Leader*, spells out the difference further. "The manager administers, the leader innovates, the manager focuses on systems and structure, the leader focuses on people. The manager relies on control, the leader inspires trust. The manager has a short range view, the leader has long range perspectives. The manager asks how and when, the leader asks what and why. The manager has his eyes always on the bottom line, the leader has his eyes on the horizon. The manager imitates, the leader originates. The manager accepts the status quo, the leader challenges it. The manager is a classic gold soldier, the leader is his own person. The manager does things right, the leader does the right thing."

Managers are necessary, but leaders are essential.

From Leader To Great Leader
You may be asking, "What has all this got to do with me? How can I inspire others? How can I make myself and others better?"

I believe that every one of us has the potential to be a great leader, and here's the key. When you are leading other people, when you are showing the way, when you are mobilising and strengthening people, when you are helping them to achieve their tasks, you are inevitably stretching yourself to go further as well. And the further you go, the further you can lead others. Leaders and followers advance towards the dream together.

To become a better leader than you are now, consider the following check list.

1. Great leaders understand that some qualities are not transferable.

You can't borrow them from others. They must be yours. Courage is not transferable. Vision is not. Understanding people are more important than profit is not. Having the persistence to stay on course through every obstacle is not. These are special qualities that you will need to cultivate yourself as you reach for your goal.

2. Great leaders create and innovate, inspire and release.

Think about the ways you're doing things now. What more creative, resourceful ways are there to do them? Perhaps you're already working with a very good system. Can it be refined or improved even further? Or can your use of that system change for the better?

3. Great leaders have to be out in front, determined to excel.

Maybe not outside the area of their gifts, but

definitely in their given task and role.

For example, I am not a gifted singer or musician, but I can speak, motivate and challenge. In Youth Alive other people sing, play instruments and dance, and they are brilliant at it.

If I tried to excel in those areas I'd be a miserable failure. But the same principles of excellence that I use to develop my gifts I can apply to the lives of others so that they can excel with their gifts. The overall result is that Youth Alive achieves a high level of excellence.

4. Great leaders are the people who strive for betterment.

They learn from others but they are still originals. They are followers, because every great leader has been a follower, but they are unique. There is something about them that is different from everyone else.

5. Great leaders are genuinely interested in people, not just structures.

They don't demand trust based on control (which is "Old School" thinking) but earn it on the basis of the respect and trust they demonstrate towards others. Their determination, faith, vision and courage earn them the right to be heard and looked up to.

6. Great leaders see the Big Picture and know exactly how necessary the whole team is to achieving that distant dream.

They take their eyes off the bottom line and focus on the horizon, seeing the unlimited resources and possibilities that await them and their team.

7. Great leaders never accept the status quo.

Average is not acceptable. Mediocre is unbearable. We talk about Lincoln, King and the other "world shakers"; they never tolerated second best. The status quo became their enemy, something to be conquered.

Being a leader means more than rocking the boat. It means tipping it over if necessary and building a new one - a better one. Remember Ben Lexcen's winged keel that helped Australia win the America's Cup? It was something radically new in yachting, the result of a pioneering spirit.

So, as a leader or potential leader, get those sails up, catch the winds of opportunity and set yourself on a course of destiny and betterment.

Wanted: Leaders With Vision
In his book *Visionary Leadership*, Bert Nanus states: "Great visionary leaders like Abraham Lincoln and Martin Luther King have been those who have been able to develop a unique vision that attracts

> *If you want to be better, be a leader.*

commitment, inspires people, revitalises organisations and mobilises the resources needed to turn vision into reality. Modern leaders know that there is no more powerful engine for driving an organisation than an attractive, worthwhile, achievable vision of the future that is widely held."

Warren Bennis lists the following ingredients as paramount in great leadership:

A guiding vision.

Passion.

Integrity.

Trust.

Curiosity.

Daring.

I believe the world needs a generation of leaders like that. Pioneers who are constantly intent on breaking through. Visionaries who dream dreams and never give them up. Men and women who love what they do with a passion and do it with ruthless honesty. Leaders prepared to learn as much as they can, and give as much as they can, and experiment and dare and risk as much as they can.

Face adversity, kick it in the teeth, follow your destiny, build life-changing qualities and you will become that leader!

Congratulations on making the right choice for your life. No matter what winds of adversity may be blowing against you today, take the time to find out what your purpose is and then give it everything you've got. Don't stop for anything. Change if change is required. Keep your focus on the dream. Move on with a spirit of excellence; mediocrity and "being average" are your enemies. Even when it feels like you're going through hell, don't stop, because on the other side are rewards that are definitely worth the effort.

DREAMERS NEVER SLEEP! GO FOR IT!

TAKE ACTION

1. Do you have any followers? If not, why not?

2. Ask yourself: "Am I leading to the best of my ability?"

3. List five people you can influence right now.
-
-
-
-
-

A QUICK LOOK AT LEADERSHIP

1. Leaders are absolutely vital to our society.

2. Leaders have vision and passion.

3. Leaders have people following them and believing in them.

4. Leaders empower and train up others giving them a sense of destiny. They are relateable and real.

5. Leaders are daring pioneers, trail blazers.

6. Leaders build teams, develop trust and inspire people to achieve.

7. Leadership is much more than management.

8. Leaders seek excellence. Status quo is their enemy.

BIBLIOGRAPHY

Pg.	Author	Title (Publisher)
27	Waitley, Denis	Empires Of The Mind (Morrow Publishing)
28	Ziglar, Zig	Over The Top (Thomas Nelson)
59	Maxwell, John C	Be A People Person (Scripture Press)
62	Mother Theresa	A Simple Path (Rider Press)
90	Waitley, Denis	Being Your Best (Audio Book-D Waitley)
93	Peale, Norman Vincent	The Power Of Positive Thinking (Simeon & Shuster)
105	Mandela, Nelson	The Long Walk To Freedom (Macdonald Purnell)
108	Sneider, Dowd & Morse Houghton	Vision, Values & Courage (The Free Press)
120	Kiev, Ari	Strategy For Divine Living (The Free Press)
134	Waitley, Denis	Empires Of The Mind (Morrow Publishing)
197	Engstrom, Ted W	The Pursuit Of Excellence (Zondervan)
247	Riley, Pat	The Winner Within (GP Putnam's Sons)
255	Gardner, John W	No Easy Victory
260	Engstrom, Ted W	ThePursuit Of Excellence (Zondervan)
262	Bennis, Warren	On Becoming A Leader (Addison Wesley)
265	Nanus, Bert	Visionary Leadership (Jossey-Bass)
266	Bennis, Warren	On Becoming A Leader (Addison Wesley)

Pat Mesiti is Director of Youth Alive NSW, in Australia, a youth organisation committed to seeing the lives of many tens of thousands of teenagers changed for the better. Each Youth Alive rally draws in excess of ten thousand people.

In addition, Pat speaks to over a quarter of a million students, youth and businesspeople every year at campuses and conferences.

Pat is a dynamic communicator who relates to people from the heart, often moving his audience from laughter to tears...and back to laughter. Through his passion and dedication to empowering and impacting the lives of young people he has gained great credibility with community leaders, civil leaders and church leadership around the world.

Pat lives in Sydney, Australia, and is married to Elizabeth. They have two daughters, Rebecca and Chantelle.

RESOURCE MATERIALS ORDER FORM

Pat Mesiti's international speaking career provides you with valuable resources that will empower you to achieve greater success in life. If *Dreamers Never Sleep* has helped you discover your dream and unlock your potential, then place your order for Pat's other outstanding tapes and books - valuable aids to you and your family's future.

For more information on products by Pat Mesiti complete the order form below and *phone/fax or mail your order today...or contact PMM direct.*

P M M
P.O. Box 1165 Castle Hill NSW 2154 Australia
PH Int + 61 2 899 6713 or 634 7633
FX Int + 61 2 899 3740

Please rush me the following tapes and books:

(indicate quantity in box)

TAPES

☐	*Building Big People* (2 tape set)	AUS$20
☐	*Super Success Strategies* (3 tape set)	AUS$25
☐	*Vision, Values & Destiny* (4 tape set)	AUS$30
☐	*Wake Up & Dream* (3 tape set)	AUS$25
☐	*Sowing & Reaping* (3 tape set)	AUS$25

BOOKS

☐	*It's Only Rock 'N Roll, But...*	AUS$10
☐	*Wake Up & Dream*	AUS$15
☐	*Dreamers Never Sleep*	AUS$15

Tapes & Books Subtotal	$AUS	
Postage	$AUS	5.00
TOTAL	**$AUS**	

Name _____

Address _____

Town _____ State _____ Post Code _____

Phone _____ Fax _____

Please debit my credit card to the value of $AUS_____

○ MASTERCARD ○ VISA ○ BANKCARD

☐☐☐☐ ☐☐☐☐ ☐☐☐☐ ☐☐☐☐
Card number

_____
Expiry Date   Signature